THE FIRST
LEATHERNECKS

Don BURZYNSKI

WARRIORS PUBLISHING
GROUP

Dedication

Dedicated to my Dad, Ted Burzynski—a World War II veteran who taught me love of country and the military—and to the 241,579 Marines KIA and WIA since 1775. This is their heritage.

A lone U.S. Army bugler plays Taps at Arlington National Cemetery, March 11, 2009.

THE FIRST LEATHERNECKS
A Warriors Publishing Group book
published by arrangement with the author.

PRINTING HISTORY
Warriors Publishing Group edition/November 2011

Warriors Publishing Group
16129 Tupper Street
North Hills, California 91343
www.warriorspublishing.com

ISBN 978-0-9821670-5-2
The name "Warriors Publishing Group" and the logo
are trademarks belonging to Warriors Publishing Group

10 9 8 7 6 5 4 3 2 1

Acknowledgements

I would like to thank the archivists at the Marine Corps University and Special Collections, Quantico—especially Ken Smith-Christmas, Pat Mullen and Jim Ginther for furnishing the manuscript of Major Edwin McClellan. Vince Vaise, Park Ranger at Fort McHenry National Monument and Historic Shrine, was also very helpful with the Marines' contribution at Baltimore/Fort McHenry.

I further thank Jim Millard at www.historiclakes.org for his extensive research of the Lake Champlain/Plattsburg battlefield; Jim Parker, Illustrator, and Connie Barone at Sackets Harbor Battlefield NY State Historic Site and; Doris Dowling, Interpreter at Trail of Tears Missouri State Park, for their contributions.

Accolades also go to the members of U.S. Marine Brigade 1812 for their inexhaustible help on early Marine history; Roger Heiple for his knowledge of Marine history; Colin Murphy, with the USS Constitution Marine Guard for his indefatigable research at the National Archives; Ken Roberts for researching the battery at the White House; Bill Moss with the Naval Historical Center, Charlestown Naval Yard, on his knowledge of sea soldiers and; Steve Abolt, 7th U.S. Infantry (Cottonbalers), for his insights regarding the 1812 American forces at the New Orleans battleground.

Special thanks to Colonel Charles Waterhouse, Marine combat artist, who graciously embellished these pages with his gifted art work. His talent, coupled with his personal history as a wounded veteran at Iwo Jima, gives me the greatest respect for his skill and accomplishments throughout his Marine years.

Finally, thanks to my editor and friend of 45 years, Bob Monement, and his enormous patience with my word changes and additions.

For those readers who want to follow the Bicennential of the War of 1812, there's no better source on that subject than Bernard J. Lossing's two-volume "Pictorial Field Book of the War of 1812." He was an amazing author and illustrator in 1869, interviewing participants 54 years after the war and drawing the battle maps that have helped me to reconstruct this history.

Table of Contents

Chapter 1: The New Praetorian Guard

Under British rule, the first four regiments of American Marines were raised by Governor William Gooch of Virginia. Known as "Gooch's Marines," they were 3,000 strong and were mostly impressed men from the dregs of Virginia waterfronts. Due to severe conditions and the low strength of the men, only ten percent survived the Cartagena expedition against Spain in 1771.

During the American Revolution, the Marines' mission was five-fold: (1) to pick off British officers and cannon crews with their muskets; (2) to serve as substitutes on cannon crews; (3) to repel boarders; (4) to lead amphibious assaults and; (5) to act as a police force enforcing fire rules, rules on thievery, and proper conduct of sailors aboard ship. These Marines slept between the ship's officers and the crew to deter mutiny.

In Benedict Arnold's Lake Champlain flotilla, a distinction was drawn for the first time between sailors and Marines. In May, 1775, the sloop Interprise had 18 Marines drawn from Massachusetts militia-men.

Congress on November 10, 1775, decided to raise two battalions of Marines to "fight as sea" and mount offensive operations on shore. According to the personal notes of Major Edwin McClellan, these Marines would be available to assist other Continental forces in the invasion of the important British naval base at Halifax, Nova Scotia. It read:

> **Resolved,** That two Battalions of Marines be raised, consisting of one Colonel, two Lieutenant Colonels, two Majors, and other officers as usual in other regiments; and that they consist of an equal number of privates with other battalions; that particular care be taken, that no person appointed to office, or inlisted into said but such as are good seamen, or so acquainted with maritime affairs as to be able to serve to advantage by sea when required; that they be inlisted and commissioned to serve for and during the present war between Great Britain and the Colonies, unless dismissed by order of Congress; that they be distinguished by the names of the First and Second battalions of American Marines, and that they be considered as part of the number which the Continental Army before Boston is ordered to consist of."

The first commission as Captain of Marines went to Samuel Nicholas of Philadelphia on Nov. 28, 1775. In Lieutenant Isaac Craig's company (the only one where a muster roll exists) only eight of the 41 recruits were native-born Americans. None of them had sea experience. Like the officers, the first Continental Marines had no knowledge of sea life and naval warfare.

Eventually, the Marines received muskets and a combination of uniforms for five small companies. It wasn't until September of 1776 that the Naval Committee ordered an official uniform for the Continental Marines.

This first uniform was a short green coat with white trim, along with a white waistcoat, buff breeches, woolen stockings and black half-gaiters. Enlisted men wore round black hats with the brim pinned on one side—the musket side.

By March, 1776, four new Marine officers were appointed to captain new ships. The brig *Lexington* was one of the first two ships, with Capt. John Barry selected for command.

On April 7, 1776, Barry's *Lexington* achieved the new American Navy's first victory against a British warship, defeating the sloop *HMS Edward* in a daring battle. Capt. John Barry commended his Marines for fighting "with much courage." Fortitudine—Latin for "courage"—became the Marines' new motto and was later inscribed on their Shako plates in 1805.

On April 6, Commodore Hopkins' squadron took on a British frigate, the *HMS Glasgow*. The British ship withstood repeated broadsides due to superior gunnery and seamanship. After an hour and a half of close combat, the *Glasgow* escaped and cost the Americans nine dead, including two Marine lieutenants.

As the Continental squadron struggled to replenish crews, Marine detachments shifted from vessel to vessel.

In March of 1777, the Marine Committee ordered the construction of 13 new frigates. A new Marine officer was assigned to each frigate. Each lieutenant or captain was required to enlist from 27 to 40 enlisted men per ship, and each Marine detachment also had a drummer and a fifer for commands in battle.

The late 1770s marked a low point in American naval history and, indeed, nearly brought the demise of the Marines itself. In 1777, the frigate *Delaware* was captured in action by the British. Her Continental Marines joined their sailor comrades in incarceration aboard the notorious prison ship *Jersey* in New York harbor—a hell ship where American Marine P.O.W.s died daily of disease and starvation.

Also in 1777, Benjamin Franklin purchased three vessels in France to attack British merchant vessels near England. He sent the Continental brig *Reprisal* on cruises from Bordeaux and L'Orient. The *Reprisal* carried a full detachment of Continental Marines. Later, caught in an Atlantic storm while heading to the U.S., the *Reprisal* foundered, drowning most of its crew and all its Marines.

In 1778, the frigate *Randolph* was blown out of the water off South Carolina in a desperate battle with the British ship-of-the-line (three decks of cannon) *Yarmouth*. The Randolph's Marine detachment, commanded by Nicholas Biddle, perished along with her sailors. Another Marine detachment was lost—this time to prison—when a British squadron captured the *Alfred* during the same year.

Middle states were forming their own coast defense navies. At the new American base at Bordertown, New Jersey, Continental Marines raided British supply vessels on the Delaware River during the winter of 1777. Retaliating, the British launched a payback raid against Bordertown in May of 1778. They dispersed the American Marines and destroyed or captured nearly 40 vessels. With the exception of one American warship commissioned in 1779, the Pennsylvania Navy and Marines ceased to exist.

At the battle of Charleston, Gen. Benjamin Lincoln surrendered the American garrison of 3,400 Continentals and militiamen. Also marching into captivity went 200 South Carolina state Marines of Abraham Whipple's squadron.

In June 1780, the frigate *Trumbull* fought one of the war's severest battles. The fighting was at close range with cannon fire and musketry sweeping both decks. The *Trumbull*'s Marine detachment expended 1,200 rounds during the battle and three Marine lieutenants and a sergeant were killed.

In all, by mid-1780, seven Marine detachments had left the Continental service either by death or capture, leaving only ten detachments at sea aboard Continental vessels.

Generally recruited from state militias, the Marines played an important part in keeping state naval crews from abandoning their warships in favor of joining the privateers. With over 2,000 privateers in service, these vessels were more attractive to sailors—and no wonder. Discipline was far more relaxed aboard privateers—and the potential for prize money was much greater. On the other hand, Marines themselves saw service aboard privateers in every part of the Atlantic and fought in some of the war's fiercest sea battles. They often served as crew for taking prize ships back to the U.S. This proved that warships couldn't fight without some sort of sea soldiers for support.

One exceptional privateer was the *Snapdragon* captained by Otaway Burns along with ten seamen. With Marine Capt. Tom Barker and his 14 Marines aboard, she captured 42 English merchant vessels in three cruises, along with 300 prisoners. Her acquired cargoes sold for $4,000,000. The prize money was divided by the 26 Americans on board—the Captain getting a larger share—that came to $145,846 for each of the Marines and crew—a king's ransom at the time. The *Snapdragon* was a lucky ship that could make a man's fortune.

While it may have seemed otherwise, not *everything* went badly for the Marines during this period.

John Paul Jones, in the Ranger, cruised the Irish Sea and landed his Marines at Whitehaven and St. Mary's Isle in western England. Commanded by Marine Lieutenant Samuel Wallingford, they pillaged some forts and stole the silver service of Lord Selkirk.

On another ship of John Paul Jones, the *Bonhomme Richard* in January, 1779, the Marine detachment was reinforced by a detachment of Irish infantry from the Regiment de Walsh-Serrant of the French army. In the war's most celebrated battle, against the *Serapis*, Marines had proved indispensable. Once more, Marine musketry contributed to an American victory.

The Frigate *Boston*'s Marine detachment also deserves note as one of the few Marine units that performed its duties—sentry watch and musketry in battle—according to ship's regulations.

Though the Continental Marines had initially been formed in 1775, for the aforementioned attack on Halifax, that mission never materialized and they were disbanded after the Revolutionary War. The rebirth of the now named United States Marine Corps was signed into being on July 11, 1798 by President Adams to fight the quasi-war with France.

The U.S., caught in the middle of the war between England and France, saw hundreds of American ships seized by the French Directory who claimed that the Americans were trading illegally with Britain.

The Frigate Act of 1794 called for the building of six vessels to include a Marine detachment of one officer and between 44 and 54 enlisted men, or roughly one Marine guard for each cannon. The idea came from British gun crews having one Marine posted to each cannon to deter sailors from abandoning their gun in horrific battle. They were to be the police onboard at sea. The Marines were now under the newly created Department of the Navy instead of the War Department.

The newly established Marine Corps enlisted men to be true volunteers. They were to be native Americans between the ages of 18 and 40, and at least five feet, six inches tall, of "robust health and sound in…Limbs and Body," and to serve for one year.

The act provided a kind of new Praetorian Guard in that the President, as Commander-in-Chief, could utilize the Marines on shore as needed or as he saw fit.

Section 6 of the July, 11 Act stated: "And, be it further enacted that the marine corps, established by this act, shall, at any time, be liable to do duty in the forts and garrisons of the U.S., on the sea coasts, or any other duty on shore, as the President, at his discretion, shall direct."

The Corps of Marines was to provide 32 detachments of ships' guards: one Major Commandant to run the Corps, 32 captains and lieutenants, 48 sergeants and corporals, 720 privates, 32 fifers and 32 drummers. Once again, a drummer and fifer were needed on board to signal battle commands.

The pay was set at $50 and four rations for the Commandant; for a captain, $40 and three rations; a 1st lieutenant, $30 and three rations; a 2nd lieutenant, $25 and two rations. Enlisted men's pay ranged from $9 for sergeants to $6 for privates. Musicians received $7. The Commandant was allowed a staff consisting of an adjutant, a paymaster, a quartermaster, a sergeant-major, a quartermaster sergeant, and a fife and drum major on shore.

The act also stipulated that when the Marines were ashore they followed the Articles of War (ergo Army regulations) and when at sea were to follow Navy regulations! This double concept was to plague the Marines for centuries as one service would covet them for duty over the other. It wasn't resolved until 1944, when the Marines were returned to the Navy. In truth, the Marines functioned under neither the Army nor the Navy—and this ambiguity resulted in their Presidential duty in Washington. The American citizens were distrustful of standing armies so the Marines by default became the only "soldiers" suitable for the Capital.

Until the end of World War II, the Marines always had a hard time maintaining their existence. They were constantly at ends with either the Navy or the Army over petty differences. The Army disliked the fact that they had to pay for lodging Marine guards at the shipyards. The Navy sea captains resented the Marine officers acting as police officers and objected to their "easier" duties on board. At other times, various Congressmen tried to abolish the Corps but were defeated by vote of Congress.

President Jefferson, in March of 1801, wanted a Marine location within marching distance of the Capital so that a few companies of Marines could defend the Capital and the Navy Yard. They were to be "troops in residence." The President used them to quell riots in the city, especially during elections. They were also needed during Shay's Rebellion, the Whiskey Rebellion, the Indian troubles, against the

Barbary pirates, and against Great Britain and France. Before the Civil War these Marines—being the closest troops available—were sent to Harper's Ferry, Maryland, to quell John Brown's raiders who were attacking the Federal arsenal there. The Marines were led by then U.S. Army Lieutenant Colonel Robert E. Lee along with his aide, Lieutenant J.E.B. Stuart.

Later in the nineteenth century, the "Guard's" role was expanded to include enforcing distillery laws, guarding National expositions, protecting American interests and businesses world-wide, avenging American citizens killed in foreign countries and guarding U.S. embassies abroad. The twentieth century brought the Foreign Service Act of 1947, formally assigning Marines to embassy duty, and the guarding of Presidential aircraft.

Although John Adams was the father of the Corps in the Revolution, and today Captain Samuel Nicholas is considered the first official Commandant, the first Commandant with the rank of Major was William Burrows, a staunch Federalist. He was the biggest contributor to the *esprit de corps* and set the Marines' high standards. He laid the splendid foundation for the new Corps that continues to present day. His first HQ was in a tent in Philadelphia, but later his HQ was moved, to avoid the perils of that city, to Washington in July of 1800. He, along with the President, picked the site for the Marine barracks at 8th and I Street which remains there to this day. (Legend has it that the British refrained from torching these barracks during the burning of Washington in honor of the Marines' heroic stand at Bladensburg, but actually they approached nowhere near that part of town.)

Burrows' immediate problem was to find soldiers fit enough for this future elite military unit. Most recruits came from Northern port cities or the Mid-Atlantic and Southern tide-water areas where recruiting stations were set up in ten cities. Finding men of "sobriety and fidelity" was not easy. He prohibited blacks, Indians, and mulattoes from enlistment. They had to be "smart, handsome and young" to fit with his epitome of military decorum. A physical exam was required with a bounty of ten dollars given upon favorable completion. Wives were allowed to accompany their husbands on land in exchange for laundry work.

Recruiting officers were expected to do everything—provide housing, rations, laundry, uniforms, arms, interviews by surgeon, measures, registration, muster rolls, size rolls, pay rolls, clothing returns, drilling and discipline and "Marining" a ship.

The complexion of each recruit was well observed. The color of his eyes and hair and any marks on his body were noted on the muster roll. He also had to give up his civilian clothing. All this was done in case of desertion—so they would have a thorough description with which to hunt him down.

Discipline was strict. Most infractions handed out a dozen lashes with the "cat of nine tails." (The term "the cat is out of the bag" stems from this punishment.) A court martial merited a maximum of 100 lashes. Desertion was punishable by death. A heroic sergeant, James Bird who fought on the Lawrence, was executed by firing squad after the battle of Lake Erie because he deserted from the Niagara—he actually missed that boat because of his girlfriend and had in fact caught the next ship out with the squadron.

A red hot branding iron with a "D" for desertion was branded on the forehead of a deserter. A "T" for thief was for a soldier caught pilfering his mess mates' possessions.

In 1801, the budget for the Corps was set at $166,903.78 and the rules on prize money were changed to give a larger share to the Marine officer who was more exposed in action. After the battle of Lake Erie, the captured British squadron sold for $242,250 in prize money. The money was divided by 596 officers, seamen and Marines who took part in the battle in proportion to their rank. Commodore Perry received $7,140—a fortune at that time—and a Marine received $214.59. Slain Marines' shares were given to their parents. Pensions were the same as given to Army and Navy personnel.

It cost $25 to uniform a Marine with one coat, one hat, one vest, two pairs of overalls, two pairs of linen overalls, four dark or checkered shirts, four shirt ruffles, four pairs of shoes, one neck stock with clasp (the ubiquitous "leatherneck"), and one blanket. A watch coat was shared by two Marines on watch along with a .75 caliber musket, a bayonet, knapsack, and cartridge box.

A sea service musket was a shorter musket so it was easier to load among the ships' rigging. It usually was a 3rd India model British Brown Bess—a very reliable weapon with interchangeable parts. Winter uniforms (wool overalls and wool long gaiters) were changed to summer uniforms (linen overalls and Russian duck gaiters) at the summer solstice and back to winter garb upon the winter equinox. The blue dress coat was worn year long even in battle with a roundabout canvas coat as a fatigue garment in camp. Any other accouterments such as canteens and haversacks for land marches were requisitioned from the Army and then returned to them.

Later, Marine officers wore the Egyptian design Mameluke sword with a four-pointed cross guard in honor of Lieutenant O'Bannon who was awarded it from Hamet Bashaw during the Marines famous march "to the shores of Tripoli." The sword was ordered in quantity from England in 1825. The same sword design is worn by Marine officers even today in memory of that heroic episode in Marine history. In another homage to Tripoli, Marines would powder each others' queue with rancid flour in two ranks. During the War of 1812, they were the only troops still wearing out-dated powdered hair. It was a form of unit citation for Tripoli.

Two chests were allowed on board—one for arms and the other for ammunition. Grenades were pulled aloft in a kedge bucket. Tents were also issued.

Six Navy yards were established with Marine guards at Portsmouth, Maine; Charlestown, Massachusetts; Philadelphia; Brooklyn; Washington and Norfolk, Virginia. Each was engaged in building frigates—the new battleships of their day. Frigates were faster than the heavy three-decked English ship-of-the-line. They were cheaper to build and had the speed to overtake their prey and to escape from an unexpectedly tough opponent. They were also tougher, with their eight inches of live oak hull sides, compared to the worm-worn wood on English ships. The American Navy started racking up victory after victory—so many that the British Admiralty decreed that a single British ship was not allowed to do battle with an American frigate by itself!

Marine duties on board now consisted of guarding P.O.W.s, guarding frigates under construction, and guarding government property. They were sentries on board and rendered honors when visiting foreign ships and ports of call. The new American Navy was very proud to display the Marines' uniform and their impeccable drill every chance they got. The uniform closely mirrored the American colors with its blue coat, red trim and white belts. The Marines manned revenue cutters on the Great Lakes as well, where smuggling was rampant.

At sea, they provided landing parties, boarding parties and repelled boarders. In close combat on a frigate, they repelled boarders by putting up an inverted U-shaped net and when the enemy crawled onto the net, the Marines speared them off with eight-foot boarding pikes.

On ships, Marines helped the seamen haul sails, scrape decks, coil cables and often acted as bargemen. They were especially helpful in winding the capstan while weighing anchor. They were not required to do this, but it made for better rapport with the Navy—and it made for good exercise. The Navy appreciated all their efforts though Marine officers drew the line at having their men go aloft to work the sails.

In battle, the Marines' main function was to provide firepower against the enemy. They fired from the poop deck and from various assigned positions on the ship. They also fought on the fighting tops—a platform above the main mast—with several Marines loading and passing the muskets to their crack marksman who did the firing. Marines to this day pride themselves on their marksmanship no matter what their duty. They also lobbed grenades from "the tops" at gun crews and at powder hatches that lay open to the powder magazine. An enemy ship could be blown sky high by one well-lobbed Marine grenade that fell into the enemy's magazine.

Marines could wait on Marine officers but not on Navy officers. Twenty cents a month was deducted from their pay for the Navy Hospital fund. On long cruises—two years—a Marine's family received one-half of the Marines pay in his absence. Rations' cost varied from 15.5 cents per day to 18.5 cents. A ration consisted of one and a quarter pounds of meat, 18 ounces of flour or bread, and one gill of spirits. Also issued were two quarts of salt, four quarts of vinegar, four pounds of soap, and one and one-half pounds of candles per 100 rations.

The Marine Corps, thanks to the foresight of Commandant Burrows, was now well on its way to becoming the elite fighting force of the United States.

The President's Own Band

When President Adams signed the Act of Congress on July 11, 1798 reestablishing the Marine Corps, it also authorized "a drum major, a fife major, and 32 drums and fifes." A $10 bounty was given to obtain hard-to-find musicians with an additional $300 anted up by Marine officers. The Band was primarily used for recruiting flourishment with the uniform to be of reverse colors—red uniforms with blue facings.

The first band's leader was William Farr and they played at the Fourth of July celebration organized by the Society of Cincinnati—a veterans' club composed of American Revolutionary War officers. By 1800, Farr added oboes, clarinets, French horns, and bassoons to the ensemble that played on New Year's Day.

Because President Jefferson loved music, he became the mentor of the Marine Band, enlarged it, and it became known as "The President's Own Band." They played at his inauguration and have continued that tradition to this day. They also continue to play each New Year's Day and on Independence Day in Washington.

As part of the enlargement of the band, the Marines based in Italy during the Tripoli fight were ordered to enlist Italian musicians in 1803. 16 Italians and their families were imported into the Corps to play. Their wives got $8 each in bounty to coerce them into leaving, in addition to the husband's bounty. Gaetano Carusi and his sons Samuel and Iznazio led the group that signed a three-year contract that ended up lasting only a year and a half.

One enlistee, Venerando Pulizzi, rejoined and stayed with the band for 21 years and eventually was leader of the band until 1827. Members of the band took part in the battle of Bladensburg and helped save Marine records during the burning of Washington.

In 1841, "Hail to the Chief" became the official tune when the President made an appearance. In July 1861, President Lincoln signed legislation which officially recognized the Marine Band by law. Lincoln's all-time favorite tune was "Dixie." Lincoln rode with the Marine Band on the train to Gettysburg for the dedication of the National Cemetery in 1863.

The band's most famous prolific director, John Phillip Sousa, of Portuguese ancestry, composed the march "Semper Fidelis" in 1888, dedicated to the Marine Corps. In 1987, President Reagan signed legislation making Sousa's, "The Stars and Stripes Forever" our official national march. After two hundred years, the band evolved into a world-class symphonic icon.

Placing the Marine Barracks, Washington, D.C.   Artist: Colonel Charles H. Waterhouse, USMCR

Visit the Marine Barracks at 8th and I Streets: www.marines.mil/unit/barracks/pages/welcome.aspx
Protocol office: 202/433-4073

Chapter 2:
Marines' First Amphibious Assault

At the onset of the American Revolution, Congress—especially the New England delegates—insisted on a Continental fleet. The Southern delegates balked at the idea but then approved it, *if* the fleet's first mission would be an incursion on the British Bahamas. New Providence, the Bahamian capital, was known to have a huge arsenal of artillery, 200 barrels of black powder, and sundry military equipment.

Commodore Hopkins, Commander of the American Fleet, had two converted merchantmen: the *Alfred*, mounting twenty 9-pounders and ten 6-pounder cannon and; the *Columbus*, armed with eighteen 9-pounders and ten 6-pounders. Two brigs, the *Andrea Doria* and the *Cabot*, had sixteen 6-pounders and fourteen 6-pounders respectively. The sloop *Hornet* mounted ten 4-pounders and the schooner *Wasp* had eight 2-pounders. All told, the fleet could fire 578 pounds of iron cannonballs per salvo.

Marine Captain Samuel Nicolas commanded the 234 Marines on board the six ships. The larger ships had a detachment of 60 Marines and the smaller ships held 20 to 40 Marines fighting as sea soldiers. He was assisted by 1st Lieutenant Matthew Parke and Lieutenant John Fitzpatrick. The Marine uniform now consisted of a light brown coat with skirts turned back and faced with white cuffs. The coat, adorned with buttons, was worn over a white cloth jacket and breeches, blue stockings and new shoes.

In early 1776, the American fleet set sail for the Bahamas from the Delaware Capes in the Philadelphia area. Nassau was the administrative center of the islands with a defense of 300 provisional militia commanded by Major Robert Sterling. The Americans anchored 50 miles north of Nassau.

Browne, the governor of the island, did nothing for defense. Fort Nassau and Fort Montagu more or less protected the city on the west and east end. Nassau had forty-six 12- and 18-pounders but they were mounted on rotten gun carriages and the fort itself had very weak walls. Montagu, more of a redoubt, had seventeen 12- and 18-pounders. With these two forts, the British considered the island its strongest possession in North America.

Commodore Hopkins determined that the two sloops and the *Providence* would surprise the town while the other ships were kept out of sight. The Marines were issued muskets, ammunition and broadswords. They were kept hidden below deck until embarking for the amphibious assault.

On Sunday, March 3, at hearing of the fleet nearby, the Governor sounded the alarm by firing three cannon, which promptly collapsed on their mounts. The gunpowder was quickly ordered to be removed to the mainland.

John Paul Jones, then captain of the *Alfred*, had the idea to land at Hanover Sound. In whaleboats, 50 sailors and 234 Marines landed at New Guinea, a freeman's port two miles east of Fort Montagu. The landing was unopposed. The British militia asked the Marines their purpose. The Marines replied: "Sent by the Congress of the United Colonies in order to possess themselves of the Powder & Stores belonging to His Majesty."

The British meanwhile had spiked all the cannon except three guns. This would have been the perfect spot to resist the Americans, but the moment was lost. The British retreated to Fort Nassau and asked their black slaves to fight alongside them. A few agreed and were armed with pistols. Marine Lieutenant John Trevett, under a flag of truce, said to the townspeople that they were coming only for the stores and would spare the town. The Marines slept that night at Montagu while Commodore Hopkins issued a manifesto to the townspeople. That night, because of the weak gun carriages, 162 barrels of powder were shipped out on the *Mississippi Packet* and the *St. John* to the Governor at St. Augustine, Florida. But, by neglecting to secure the west door of the city, Commodore Hopkins failed to get all the powder.

The next day, the Marines took Fort Nassau without firing a shot. The grand flag of the United Colonies was run up in place of the British colors. Capt. Dayton and Lt. Trevett captured the Governor, who appeared ready to escape. With the Governor prisoner, the 32-man Marine guard used at their discretion all the Governor's wine and other liquors as they did everything else for which they had occasion. The Governor wouldn't go aboard the *Alfred* so he was seized, collared and dragged away. He and two other officials were later returned and paroled.

The American ships were loaded with the captured munitions. The *Andrea Doria* received 4,780 shot and shells to replace her stone ballast which was dumped on shore. Hopkins set up a triangle on the capital parade ground where inhabitants could make complaints against any of his men, who were punished immediately if found guilty. His courts martial were short and decisive with the number of lashes few but very severely given.

The Marines captured a total of 46 iron cannon, 140 hand grenades, 9,831 rounds of shot, 154 bolts of double-headed shot (a high-tech munition used for cutting rigging), 11 canisters of grape, two mortars, 24 barrels of powder, 220 gun carriages and 355 British pounds sterling.

On Saturday, March 16, the Marines embarked for home. By attacking outside of the continental U.S., the Americans had internationalized the war. British supremacy on the sea, as well as other British enclaves ranging from the West Indies to Canada, were now challenged by the Americans and found themselves open to a possible Marine amphibious assault anywhere. The Revolution had taken on a new dimension.

The First Landing   Artist: Colonel Charles H. Waterhouse, USMCR

Visit the battle site: www.hiltoncaribbean.com/index.php?destination-nassau

Chapter 3:
Marines Leave Their Ships for Princeton

After the victory at Trenton, NJ on Dec. 25, 1776, George Washington let General Lord Cornwallis pursue him from his base at Princeton. Even though the Americans were outnumbered three to one, this presented an opportunity for Washington, for while Cornwallis was moving on them, their base, with stores of munitions, would be vulnerable to attack. At night, with rail campfires burning brightly, the U.S. force took a southern road to the east while the British marched west.

The American army formed in two attacking columns. General Mercer and Brigadier General Calwalader's brigade, with 600 U.S. Marines and Pennsylvania state Marines pulled from various ships in Philadelphia: The *Delaware, Effingham, Washington, Virginia, Andrea Doria, Champion, Montgomery* and the Pennsylvania ships *Hancock* and *Defence*. Marine officers included Captains Porter, Mullen, Love, Montgomery, Deane, Craig, Shaw, Leary, Disney, Brown, Shippin, and Brown. All were commanded by Marine Major Sam Nicholas who, under General Greene, marched up Quaker road and were to secure the left flank.

Along with Maj. Nicholas was Captain Robert Mullen, owner of Tun Tavern, which became a legendary recruiting center for Marines. In June of 1776, Congress had approved commissions for 14 new Marine officers—among them was the tavern-owner Mullen. For the first time, American Marines marched off to bolster an American army.

General Sullivan took the Saw Mill road and was to attack Princeton from the east. The 40th regiment of foot was the only British force left in Princeton. Colonel Mawhood and the 17th regiment of foot, on the march to Trenton, caught sight of the flank of Mercer's troops. Mercer, thinking them a small scouting party, attacked Mawhood's men. Hidden behind a bank, the British rose and fired at the Americans. Their shots were all too high, thanks to the British troops being trained to close their eyes when pulling the trigger. While the Americans started their volley, the British came at them with cold steel and overpowered the Americans. Gen. Mercer was bayoneted to death and the American force fled in disorder.

The British excelled at the use of the bayonet—and their officers took great delight in closing with the Americans. One British General, "No-Flint" Grey, actually had his NCOs knock the flints out of his men's muskets before going into battle with their bayonet alone. He felt—and rightly so—that it winnowed out his weaker troops. The Americans were at a great disadvantage because they only had a scant supply of bayonets—let alone sufficient training with the weapon. Only when the French army entered the war and supplied them with Baron von Steuben training did Americans learn how to parry British "charge bayonets."

Calwalader and the Marines heard firing in the distance and marched to the guns. Seeing Mercer's men in full retreat, he formed the column in divisions to the right. Morgan's crack battalion of Virginia riflemen on the left flank with Matlock's riflemen and Nicholas' Marines on the right fired at the British, but were too far for effect. They were ordered to advance at double-time and reload on the move. They got within 50 yards of the British, who let the Marines have it with several well-trained devastating volleys. The Marines were driven back 40 yards and trying to regroup was a failure.

Then, Gen. Washington appeared and proceeded to rally the troops. Capt. Moulder's two artillery pieces began to pound the 17th —and with the arrival of Sullivan's division the situation was resolved. Colonel Hand's riflemen went against Mawhood's left while the Marines and Major Israel Angell pressed the center. With the renewed attack, the British line gave way and the 17th scattered. The 55th regiment of foot came up from Princeton, but was routed by Sullivan's Continentals.

As the Americans took the city, the 55th took up defensive positions in Nassau Hall. As legend has it, a lucky American cannonball beheaded the portrait of King George III hanging in the hall. The British, seeing this as an omen, quickly surrendered. Two British regiments were annihilated in detail attesting to Washington's prowess.

The British lost 500 dead. American losses were seven officers and 30 privates slain. Among them was the perforated body of Gen. Mercer. Also killed was Pennsylvania Marine Capt. William Shippen.

After the Trenton-Princeton campaign, the three reduced Marine companies joined Washington's army at Morristown, New Jersey, in those infamous miserable winter quarters.

 Levying Nicholas' three marine companies into the army, against the invasion of Pennsylvania, seemed to crush the idea of an independent Corps of Marines. Next came the disintegration of centralized control by the Marine Committee. Marines were, at this point, relegated to ship detachments. It was the beginning of the demise of the Corps' original *Resolve of Nov. 10, 1775*. There would follow 167 years of continuing battle with the Army and Congress as to how Marines should be used.

As we know, it was by no means the end of the U.S. Marine Corps.

Marines with Washington at Princeton   Artist: Colonel Charles H. Waterhouse, USMCR

Visit the battle site: www.state.nj.us/dep/parksandforests/parks/princeton.html

Chapter 4:
Marines Defeated at Penobscot Bay

Due to the success of American privateers capturing British shipping between New York and Halifax, the British had need of a closer base for launching patrols of their shipping lanes. They set about establishing a base in Penobscot Bay, Maine, with the further hope that a refuge and a colony might take hold, attracting Loyalists from the rebelling colonies.

The Council of Massachusetts Bay asked the Navy Board of the Eastern Department for assistance in repelling the British. The British forces there were the 74th and the 82nd regiments of foot, a total of 640 men. The readied American fleet consisted of four Continental navy ships, three Massachusetts state navy ships, 12 privateers and 20 transports. Three companies of Continental and state marines under Captain Walsh, along with 1,500 militia, were assembled. Only 873 militiamen were fit to fight—and those were ill-trained.

The American fleet sailed on July 24, 1779 and found the British warships formed in a line across the entrance to Bagaduce harbor. They were protecting their half-finished fort at this site and their fleet of transports farther up the harbor. There was a steep precipice to the west of the fort, while the south was protected by cannon from inside the walls. The other two sides were inaccessible. Even so, Marine Sergeant Tom Philbrook said "the fort was only three and a half feet high which our men could straddle over without much difficulty." The fort had two cannon in *barbette* with *chevaux-de-frise* on the ramparts. The British had removed their ships' starboard cannon and placed them in the fort, on the mainland, and on other peninsulas.

The 60 Marines under Capt. Walsh were ordered to land and take possession of Banks Island at the entrance of the river. The 1st division was to land on the opposite side of the peninsula. Twenty British marines retired leaving four artillery pieces. Under cover of night, the Americans set up two 18- and one 12-pounder cannon. On Tuesday, the island was secured in a brilliantly executed maneuver. By capturing the island, the British were forced to move their ships farther up the bay to escape battery fire.

Disagreement then arose between the naval and army commanders. The Army wanted the British ships attacked. The Navy didn't want to attack while under the guns of the fort and insisted the assault was to begin on the precipitous cliffs. The Navy refused to talk about the matter anymore, and relegated further discussion to junior officers. At a council of war, it was determined that the Army and Marines were to proceed with the landing before the attack on the enemy ships would begin.

Eight hundred fifty militia and 227 Continental and state marines—with 80 of Colonel Paul Revere's cannoneers—were in the 1st division. The Marines were on the right with the left composed of the Cumberland County regiment. The 2nd division, the Lincoln County militia with Revere's men, was to be held in reserve. The troops were tired and had low morale from waiting in cramped, standing-room-only ships. Forty-five ships were lined parallel to the shore giving fire into the woods to "scour the enemy."

At first light, the boats approached the shore. The Marines were supposed to form in line of battle, but the perpendicular precipice made them climb in groups, unable to return fire, because both hands were needed to climb the cliff. The Marines met the stiffest resistance, especially from the harbor battery firing at close range. Capt. Walsh was killed and Lt. William Hamilton was severely wounded. Thirty-two Marines were killed or wounded here.

Then, Sattonstall decided not to attack the British ships! The land force stopped before reaching the fort, afraid of flanking fire from the British ships. Commodore Sattonstall had hesitated and retreated after only one of his ships was hit. He was definitely not the forceful commander this assault needed.

The Americans surrounded the fort with cannon but went into a defensive posture, their morale very low. Sattonstall would not attack the British ships until the fort was taken—and the Army wouldn't attack the fort till after Sattonstall's ships had engaged—so a command stalemate ensued. For three weeks, nothing happened.

A new British squadron of seven ships appeared with 1,530 experienced and heavily armed men. The American ships were defeated, their fleet either fled into small tributaries or scuttled by their own crews. The Marines, sailors and militia fled through the woods, all of the 200 miles to Boston, mostly on foot.

By September, troops were filtering back into Boston with their account of the botched attack. Commodore Sattonstall was found guilty at court martial and declared unfit to command a Continental vessel. Not only was the expedition a failure, but it was a financial disaster for Massachusetts, which lost 11 million pounds sterling—and its entire fleet in Maine.

Overall, this was a demoralizing defeat with a direct impact on subsequent amphibious operations. It was not until the Mexican War, 68 years later, that Marines would again attempt to launch a sizable amphibious operation. The defeat had been caused by a divided command, poor planning, poorly trained forces and lack of aggressive leadership. However, the successful occupation of Banks Island and gaining the heights at Bagaduce attested to the Marines' bravery and determination.

Assault at Penobscot   Artist: Colonel Charles H. Waterhouse, USMCR

Visit the battle site: www.penobscotmaritimemuseum.org

Chapter 5:
The March "to the Shores of Tripoli"

In 1805, the fledgling United States sent just eight Marines to invade a wild and hostile nation that is now Libya. The mission entailed a five hundred and twenty mile march from Alexandria, Egypt, to the city of Derne in what would become one of the most glorious and triumphant stories in Marine Corps history.

This region of North Africa was particularly treacherous for Western travelers and well-deserved the name "Barbary Coast." For centuries, the European powers had paid tribute to the Barbary States to protect their richly laden commercial vessels. Piracy had been a main occupation here for over 11 centuries and was condoned by the Moslem faith. Over a million Christians had been taken from ships and the men sold into slavery as galley oarsmen or construction gangs. The women, especially if they were blond and blue-eyed, were sold into harems at the slave auction. U.S. ships were especially vulnerable since, having just won independence from England, America had lost the protection of the British fleet. The Arabs referred to these ships as "fat ducks."

On October 31, 1803, the frigate *Philadelphia* ran aground in Tripoli's harbor. The 41 Marines and 268 crew aboard had been enslaved by the Tripolians and were in mortal danger. As Christians, they were treated even more harshly than the Arabs' Moslem prisoners. If a seaman was even slightly disrespectful of the Moslem faith, he was either roasted alive, impaled or crucified. For the murder of a Mohammedan, a prisoner would be cast over the city wall to be caught on iron hooks halfway down—where he would hang in agony for several days before dying. After nearly a year-and-a-half of such jeopardy, it became a matter of urgency for the Marines to free their brothers-in-arms.

William Eaton, an ex-Army Captain and special envoy of President Jefferson, had devised a plan to replace Yousif Bashaw, the ruler of Tripoli, with his brother Hamet. A ruler friendly to the United States would save millions in tribute and would allow our merchant ships to sail the Mediterranean Sea without fear of Tripolian pirates and ransoms. Jefferson approved the plan and named Eaton a general, specifically for the purpose of the adventure. With the advent of the *Philadelphia* incident, time was of the essence.

"General" Eaton commandeered Marine Lieutenant Presley O'Bannon, Sergeant Campbell and Privates O'Brian, Thomas, Owens, Whittier, and Stewart, whose main duty on the march was to guard the food supply and the war chest. They led a composite force of 300 superb Arab horsemen led by Sheiks Mahomet and el Tahib, 70 Christian mercenaries, 25 cannoneers led by Selim Comb (a janizary), 38 Greek mercenaries led by Grecian Captains Ulofic and Constantine, plus a baggage train of 107 pack camels. The march was to be a test of survival in the hot sands of the Sahara desert complicated by constant problems from the Arabs who were supposed to be part of the team effort.

Normally, a Marine operation would attack from sea to the shore, but in this case the attack would come *from* the desert *to* the shore. So this original special ops army marched 20 miles a day for seven weeks and cut through the dry desert far from the sea. They lived on two biscuits a day, rice, and water worse than bilge swill. Some Bedouins later showed them how to eat wild fennel roots and sorrel leaves. For meat, they ate camels, sheep and, in one instance, a wildcat caught by a trained greyhound.

The march began right during the *Khamsin*, or sandstorm season. Starting after the spring equinox, one huge storm lasted for 50 days with fine sand entering everything, especially the food. On the second day, the Arabs refused to march because Eaton's earlier payment had no timeframe, so the Arabs demanded more money "now and then." The Marines had to dig into their own pockets to pitch in for payment.

The search for water was constant. If they were lucky, the group would sometimes find natural cisterns formed by rain water cascading onto solid rock since Hannibal's days. When the army reached the old Carthaginian ruin of Masouah, the resident sheik sold cattle, sheep, goats, fowl, skins of butter, dates and milk to the thirsty, starving column. The Marines drank the date wine while the Muslims wouldn't touch the alcohol. Intel came in reporting an 800 cavalry enemy reinforcement strengthening Derne. Eaton sent a message to the American fleet stationed at Tripoli asking for 100 more Marines and bomb ships, but the request was denied. His sparse army would eventually need to attack the fortress at Tripoli where the 300 American sailors and Marines of the *Philadelphia* were in slavery after having surrendered without a fight.

The Bashaw of Tripoli, hearing of the approaching army, asked a foreign envoy how many Marines the U.S. had. When told "thousands," he was more afraid of them than of all the American ships. He said, "Though they are gentlemen, they fight like lions." A messenger informed the column that Commodore Hull was on the way with the ship *Argus*, 7,000 Spanish dollars and supplies, headed to rendezvous at Bomba. The *Argus* was to meet the column at Bomba to re-supply before the assault on Derne. She was to bring 30 hogsheads (60 three-gallon casks) of bread, 20 barrels of peas, ten tierces (40 two-gallon casks) of rice, a hogshead of brandy, two hogsheads of wine, and 100 sacks of flour in addition to the cash.

On March 22, the column came across a huge caravan of Bedouins at Oak Kerar ke Barre oasis who were willing to trade. Dates, cattle, horses, goats and ostriches were for sale. Replacement camels were bought at 11 dollars each. The Bedouins, nomads of the desert, were astonished at the Marine's blue coats and the brightness of their buttons and muskets. Next day, Lt. O'Bannon noticed that many of the Marines were missing buttons from their coatees and soon discovered they had traded the shiny "coins" for favors from Bedouin women. The Lieutenant graciously did not press charges.

The march was reinforced by recruiting 80 more Arabs mounted on magnificent Arabian horses. They now had 150 fighters bivouacked in 47 tents. But then Sheik el Tahib, a persistent malcontent, mutinied again. Hamet wanted the horses back from the Marines and el Tahib decamped once again.

The next day, the Arabs reappeared. Sheik Mahomet said he'd been cheated of his share of dollars by el Tahib in an argument that lasted all day. The Marines became convinced that the squabbling Arabs had no honor, no patriotism, and were thieves who were only motivated by their religion and by a penchant for acting hospitable. By August 8, however, the march had increased to 700 fighters and 1,200 camp followers.

For his part, Lt. O'Bannon continued to drill his riflemen on the manual of arms. One day, a crowd of Arabs watching them mistakenly thought that they were being fired upon when the command "take aim, fire" was called as a dry run. Rice was offered to the Arabs and a face-off was averted. Hamet proclaimed O'Bannon "the brave American" and presented the Lieutenant with a Mameluke sword from

Egypt which had a curved blade and a four-pointed cross guard. A version of this design is carried by Marine officers to this day, commemorating the march across the Sahara desert by "a few good men."

On the following day, the Bedouin foot soldiers gave up the march. Reaching the port of Bomba for food was now the column's rallying cry. They camped in a cultivated area of red cedars and barley. The ship *Hornet* finally showed up with the promised provisions and the Marines and Arabs revived themselves with an abundant feast—all the desert hardships were forgotten. Of course, the brandy and wine casks were opened first. The army was now ready to assault Derne on the morrow.

> **During Eaton's 520 mile march to Tripoli, Commodore Barron's U.S. naval squadron was sent to the Barbary Coast. This second enlarged fleet consisted of the *President, Constitution, Congress, Constellation, Essex, Siren, Argus, Vixen, Enterprise, Nautilus, John Adams* and the *Hornet* along with two bomb ships and 12 gun boats. Some craft patrolled along the Moorish coast while the rest maintained the blockade of Tripoli in 1804.**

The objective town of Derne was a flourishing center of date groves and irrigated fields thanks to the fresh water of *Jabel Ahdar* (Green Mountain) and the river Wadi Derne that flowed from it. The cultivated gardens of the town grew melons, grapes, figs, bananas, oranges, plums and other fruit. The rear of the town, once a thriving countryside, had been reclaimed by the wilderness of shifting sands. The harbor fortress had a water battery of eight 9-pounder cannons. The palace where Mustafa, the governor/commandant, resided was on the western side of Wadi Derne across from the main gardens and the harbor fort. The inhabitants had loop-holed the walls of the houses and terraces for defense, although only a third of the people were actually sympathetic to resist the invaders. Most of the Tripolian fighters had set up defenses in the wadi before the town.

Eaton and the Marines planned to take the fortress first since it was the strongest obstacle. The *Argus* and the *Hornet* were to bombard the fortress. The Marines needed cannon for the land assault and two brass fieldpieces were delivered to them by the *Argus*. The guns were dismantled and hauled up a 20-foot cliff to high ground over the wadi. Eaton sent smoke signals American-Indian style from the mountain to signal American ships that they were in position. The *Nautilus* under Captain Dent replied, but had no additional cannon for them. Next morning the *Argus* and the *Hornet* entered the bay for fire support. A number of sheiks from the town visited the invading camp and said that two-thirds of the town favored Hamet's cause. The governor of Derne had an 800-man defensive force, and expected a reinforcement army any day, so Eaton's American-Arab-Bedouin army had to be ready to attack as soon as Hamet's army could join up with them.

Eaton offered a peace letter to his foe in advance of the attack. Mustafa's answer was "My head or yours." On April 27, the *Hornet* commenced firing at 100 yards with eight 9-pounders. The *Nautilus* contributed 12 cannon, and the *Argus*, with 16 cannon, opened up with her 24-pounders. A total of 38 guns spewed 792 pounds of iron per salvo at the fortress walls. In one intense hour the water fort's guns were silenced.

Eaton attacked in two columns: first were the Marines, Comb's 25 mercenaries, and 38 Greek and Arab foot soldiers under Lt. O'Bannon. The second column was Hamet's 1,000 horsemen attacking from the west and southwest. They were to seize an old castle which was perfectly positioned to repel any reinforcement.

O'Bannon's artillery opened fire at 2 p.m., but a lucky Arab shot destroyed their rammer early on. The attack was almost broken—except for the Marines. At this point, the odds were ten to one against the Americans, and it seemed the Tripolians must certainly win. But Eaton, with his fiery temper and sensing failure, ordered a bayonet charge. The whole line moved forward. Eaton was shot in the left wrist, but continued to fire his rifle. Then, amazingly, Mustafa's army broke. The Marines took the ravine defensive line and pressed on to the water fort. The fortress was taken in an hour and a half and O'Bannon hoisted the American flag over the fortress—the first time American colors had ever flown over foreign soil.

The Marines wheeled around the loaded cannons they'd captured and pounded the town. Hamet's men, in a pincer movement, took the south, along with the Bey's palace, and joined the Marines in Derne. The town was theirs. The long march had paid off and the unwavering courage of Eaton and his seven Marines established a reputation enjoyed by the USMC to this day.

The American losses included 14 Christians killed or wounded and of the seven Marines, one was killed, one mortally wounded, and a third wounded. The Greeks—true to their ancient character—had fought well. Bey Mustafa had fled to the harem of one of his friends. Eaton was unable to pursue him there because harems were considered sacred and all the Arabs would have turned against him. Mustafa eventually escaped and waited for Hassen's reinforcement army.

Eaton prepared for a formidable counter-attack. The Marines fortified the fort and their Arab allies occupied the plain near the town. Within four days, Hassen Bey and his 3,000 enemy Arabs appeared, the Beys of Bengazi and Oznan and Hadgi Ismain commanding their cavalry.

Hassen attacked on May 13, on both sides of the river valley. The Arabs fought harder against each other then they had against the Americans. Hamet was once forced to retreat into the town and fought from houses and terraces. Then, after a broadside from an American ship, it was Hassen's men on the retreat. In desperation, Hassan offered 6,000 dollars for Eaton's head and tried to bait a trap by offering two beautiful Arab women for the American's pleasure. Eaton was smart enough to realize that such intrigues would end in his own poisoning.

The Christian battalion under O'Bannon then advanced from the fort into the town. The whole town cheered the blue-coated Marines, "Long live the Americans! Long live our friends and protectors!" Hassen launched a mounted attack on Hamet's cavalry outpost and a full scale cavalry battle formed involving 5,000 white-robed horsemen on their beautiful Arabian steeds. Since the horsemen from both sides were thoroughly mixed in battle, the *Argus* and the *Hornet* couldn't fire into the enemy. This battle went on for four hours, first with swords then with rifles. About forty men on each side were killed.

O'Bannon and the Marines had wanted to join the fight but Eaton refused them. Commodore Hull also witnessed the battle and sent his ship's surgeon to care for Hamet's wounded Arabs. Finally, the American frigate *Constitution* appeared and the enemy had had enough. It was the ship that broke the camel's back.

The ship brought some unbelievable news as well. Tobias Lear, another American envoy, had negotiated a treaty with Yousif, ending the war with Tripoli. He'd paid 60,000 dollars for the release of the American prisoners. The American flag was raised again in front of the U.S. consulate, where it had been before the flag pole had been chopped down. The slaves from the *Philadelphia* were released and were going home—less 30 who had died during their ordeal. By provision, Eaton had to relinquish the hard-won Derne town. Commodore Barron had not believed that the fickle Hamet could rule effectively and withdrew all support of his army. He cut off all supply of arms, money and provisions, even though Hamet was winning the fight.

The *Constellation* then appeared with orders to embark Eaton and his Marines. Eaton broke the news to Hamet who was dumbfounded in disbelief. They were almost at the point of victory and the plug was pulled!

It became necessary for Eaton to resort to subterfuge to mask his retreat. The Marines and Arabs were inspected, ammo and rations distributed and spies were sent out to reconnoiter the enemy force, as if to set up for an attack. Eaton pretended to make a move on Tripoli and positioned the Marines near the fort's wharf. The *Constellation*'s boats came in and took off the Greeks and mercenaries who had no idea what was happening. Hamet and his retinue were also taken out.

The town got wind of what going on and, as in Saigon more than a century and a half later, watched the Marines board the last boat. Townspeople rushed the boats shouting and cursing the faithless infidels with whom they had marched. Their fate was sealed. Yousif promised amnesty but the Arabs didn't believe him. They headed for the hills, infuriated.

The triumph at Derne—a saga which survives in the opening stanza of the Marine Corps hymn, in the blade and hilt of the Marine officer's sword, and as a part of the *esprit de corps* of a great fighting organization—belonged to history. The now unemployed Eaton had helped the Marine Corps to a glorious awakening.

The four-year war with Tripoli was over. Commodore Rodgers took Commodore Barron's place. American commerce was restored in the Mediterranean. Pope Pius VII declared that the United States alone had pacified the North African pirates—something all the great European powers had not been able to accomplish.

The aggressive operations of the new American Navy had impressed the world, made the U.S. a world power, and had been an admirable school for the U.S. Navy and Marines. Though the Marine Corps was established in 1795, the soul of the Corps—which made its honor and tradition ideals worth dying for—was inspired by the hot winds of a distant desert in 1805.

Assault on Derna, Tripoli   Artist: Colonel Charles H. Waterhouse, USMCR

Visit the Battlefield: www.libyantravels.com/Derna.htm

Chapter 6:
U.S. Forces Burn York (Toronto)

The War of 1812

The military forces of the United Kingdom and France were in open conflict on land and sea. While the armies of Britain fought to repel the armies of Napoleon Bonaparte, the British Navy sought to impose a naval blockade around continental Europe, intent on starving Napoleon of necessary supplies. As the young United States allied with France, it too was drawn into the conflict with the British superpower.

Many American ships were forcibly intercepted by the British Navy and their cargo and crews seized. The perceived affront to their liberty, combined with a growing conviction among many American politicians that the U.S. was destined to somehow rule the entire North American continent in a policy known as Manifest Destiny, helped solidify U.S. resentment of the growing power of the British Empire.

Hostilities increased between Britain and the U.S. and open warfare was declared by the U.S. Congress on June 18, 1812. Many Americans saw military action against British North America as a war of liberation. There was a prevailing sentiment that American forces would be freeing colonists from the yoke of British oppression and that the invasion would be concluded quickly as a "mere matter of marching."

The residents of British North America, now Canada, who mostly lived along the shores of the St. Lawrence River and the Great Lakes, thought otherwise. Since the American Revolution, 60,000 Loyalists had left the U.S., primarily for Canada. American invasion forces were met with fierce and largely successful opposition. The British military, aided by local volunteer militias and natives, fought bravely at Niagara, York and all along the frontier and were successful in defending the colony from the American onslaught.

With the opposing naval bases on Lake Ontario only 35 miles apart, the British and American fleets played cat and mouse, attempting to position themselves for an attack advantage. While the British were blockading Sackets Harbor, Commodore Chauncey slipped away to attack York, in present-day Toronto.

York had two British batteries on the east of the town with a small blockhouse. A larger blockhouse to the west, with 800 men, was commanded by Major General Roger Shaeffe. The British defenses were weak. The cannon were without trunnions and were frozen in mud. A newly built 10-gun brig, *HMS Duke of Gloucester,* was in port.

On April 27, 1813, with 1,700 soldiers and Marines, the American fleet appeared before York. The land forces were lead by General Zebulon Pike, explorer and namesake of Pike's Peak in Colorado. Chauncey's message to the fleet read, "It is expected that every corps will be mindful of the honor of the American arms and endeavor by a cool and determined discharge of their duty, to support the one and wipe off the other."

There was little support for this war among the townsfolk. The Americans thought York's populace, mostly comprised of new American settlers, would flock to the American colors—but that didn't happen. The Quebecois, or French Canadians, had been allowed by the British to keep their language, customs and culture, and didn't want to be assimilated.

The attack started at 8 a.m. with Major Forsyth and his riflemen hitting the beach first. Their landing craft had blown a half-mile to the west beyond the covering fire of the fleet and they were met by heavy volleys by the Glengarry Fencibles and Indians. The American attack column consisted of the 6th, 15th, 16th, and 21st regiments, a detachment of light and heavy artillery, and Colonel M. Clare's volunteers as flankers. The Marines were held in reserve aboard ship in case the Great Lakes fleet of Sir James Lucas Yeo appeared and there would be a ship battle. The British were reinforced by companies of the 8th Royal Newfoundland Regiment, and a large body of militia and Indians.

The British attacked the American flankers but sustained heavy losses. They were overpowered and fell back. Pike's bugler sounded the advance. The Indians were terrified by the bugle blast and gave one horrified yell as they fled into the woods.

The fleet cheered and began to fire grapeshot. The British retreated quickly to the town and the Americans struck up "Yankee Doodle" in the quick march to York. Since the bridges were destroyed, the artillerymen had hot work moving their great guns forward as they were met by British 24-pounders.

The fleet then attacked the town and commenced heavy shot fire. Over 200 pounds of iron shot per ship salvo was hurled at the British capital. The American ground forces charged with bayonets, attacking the two blockhouses and leaving them abandoned and spiked. The artillery silenced the guns of the enemy who had retreated to the town.

At that moment, the ground shook with a thunderous explosion. The British had accidentally blown their own powder magazine holding 500 barrels of gunpowder (12.5 tons). Huge timbers and stone blocks flew for hundreds of yards. Fifty-two Americans were killed and 180 wounded. Forty of the British were also killed. General Pike, crushed by a stone block, was mortally wounded. Gen. Henry Dearborn was quite ill but assumed command and, weighing over 250 pounds, was rolled about in a two-wheeled cart contraption later called a "Dearborn." He reformed the attack and, with three cheers from his men, entered the capital of Canada with its 900 inhabitants.

The sailors and Marines landed and burned York's public buildings, including the legislative chambers, because of a human scalp found over the mace behind the speaker's chair. They also burned the house of Mrs. Gwen, wife of the Indian Department leader. The Americans showed no mercy for British Indian leaders who had conjured up the Indians to fight. It was known British frontier policy to buy American scalps from the Indians for 20 pounds sterling and one British officer—Hamilton at Fort Malden—had the dubious distinction of being known as "The Hairbuyer."

Example of American scalp supposedly found on Parliament wall behind speaker's chair.
Courtesy of Benson Lossing

The American losses were 66 killed and 203 wounded. The Marine losses were 17 killed and wounded. British losses were 60 killed, 89 wounded, in addition to prisoners taken by the Americans. Pike was carried on board where he smiled at the news of the American flag raised over the town. The surrendered British flag was placed under his head and he died. His remains were preserved in a cask of spirits until he could be buried at Sackets. The British parliamentary mace taken from the capital was presented by Commodore Chauncey to the Secretary of the Navy.

The Americans captured 290 prisoners and a huge quantity of naval and military stores. The naval stores included all of the armament and equipment for the British squadron on Lake Erie as well as the stores for the new ship under construction at Amherstburg. Cables, cordage, canvas, tools, guns, and ammunition were all seized. This move seriously crippled the British right division, aiding the American victory on Lake Erie five months later.

York marked the first American victory in ten months of warfare. Pike's ability as a commander was proven as the British had been overwhelmed without putting up much of a fight. They had retreated east to Kingston to fight another day—much to the dislike of the people of that town.

The inhabitants of York were thrilled when the Americans distributed farm implements they'd found in a warehouse, along with a huge supply of peas, flour and bread that the Americans couldn't fit in their ships.

The Americans were upset that they hadn't captured the British ships. The frigate *Isaac Brock* was burned by the retreating British and her sister ship, the *Duke of Gloucester,* had slipped away. But York, intended as a ship building base, ceased to produce ships. When the British later tried shipbuilding there again, it was burned once more by the American fleet.

In retaliation, Washington City was eventually torched for the burning of the York capital buildings and for the burning of Newark. The War of 1812 was the first where *total war* was waged. For the first time, towns were burned on both sides and modern warfare had begun to take on a new "scorched earth" policy.

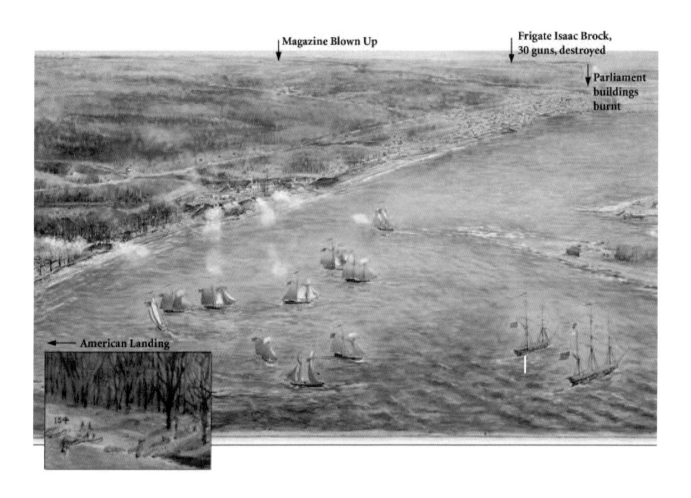

Arrival of the 16 ships of the American fleet prior to the capture of York, April 27, 1813
Courtesy of Toronto Public Library

Visit the battlefield: www.toronto.ca/culture/museums/fort-york.htm

Chapter 7: The Battle of Fort George

After destroying York, now known as Toronto, the American fleet decided to do the same at the British Fort George on Lake Ontario. Even though this fort was headquarters for the Central Division of the British Army, it had been stripped of its heaviest armament. Its big guns had been sent for the defense of Fort Malden—a strategy that was to prove disastrous for Fort George.

On May 21, 1813, with 17 warships and over a hundred Durham landing boats, an elite American attack force was assembled. The first wave consisted of 800 men from the flank companies of the 15th U.S. infantry, Lt. Col Benjamin Forsyth's battalion of riflemen, and the artillery detachment of Lt. Col. Winfield Scott (future conqueror of Mexico and of the Confederacy). The second column was Gen. Boyd's brigade of infantry, Lt. Col George McClure's rifle volunteers, with Maj. Abram Eustis' battalion of artillery. The third column was Winder's brigade with Capt. Nathan Towson's artillery and Chandler's brigade with Col. Alexander Macomb's artillery. Winder and Chandler were to form on Boyd's right and left respectively. Each brigade fielded 1,500 men making a total of 5,300 Americans in all. The Marines of the fleet and 400 carefully-picked sailors were held in reserve.

The fleet fired over the heads of the men advancing in boats until they were close enough to be sheltered by the clay bank on shore. Once over the top, the attacking force met head-on the Glengarry Light Infantry, the Grenadiers of The Royal Newfoundland Regiment, the 8th Regiment, the Lincoln militia, and Capt. Runchey's Negro Company of freed slaves. When the Americans were stopped cold, the fleet recommenced firing. Then the Americans were driven back by the bayonet, but again tried to ascend the bank. At only six yards apart, both lines fired volleys for 15 minutes. The American rifle fire was devastating. In one rectangular section of ground, measuring 15 by 200 yards, were 400 British dead and wounded. Every British officer had been hit.

Having no horses, the Americans advanced, dragging their artillery. The British artillery was able to halt the three advancing columns but the American riflemen kept advancing through the woods, outflanking the British repeatedly. The American artillery, numbering 51 cannon, then pounded the palisaded fort to smithereens.

Commodore Perry personally directed each ship's salvo onto the British formations, going from ship to ship in a jolly boat. The flagship *Madison* sailed abreast of the fort and added its hot-shot cannonade. The hot-shot, red hot cannonballs that had been heated to set a target on fire, was devastating. Nothing was left of the wooden fortress except smoldering toothpicks.

The Americans encircled the entire area and advanced on the Queenston road where British reinforcements were expected. The fort was captured and the village of Newark was heavily shot up by cannon fire. The British retreated down the Queenston road, destroying their Fort Erie and all the works up to Chippawa.

The British lost 52 killed, 44 wounded and 262 missing. American losses were 150 wounded and missing with 39 killed. Most losses were in line formation, 45 feet from each other. Army Maj. Gen. Henry Dearborn, already ill, was further enfeebled during the fight. Col. Scott, a magnificent warrior at six-and-a-half feet tall, had been everywhere, directing the attack. He personally doused the charge that the British had set to blow their magazine. He also chopped down the British flagpole, capturing their flag. Later, he was unhorsed, suffering a broken collarbone caused by a large splinter.

After the battle, the American militia—especially Forsyth's—became disorderly, pillaging and burning the town of Newark, present day Niagara-on-the-Lake. They were retaliating for the burning of their town—Ogdensburg in upstate New York. Perry led the sailors and the Marines onto the beachhead, calling on the Marines to stop the looting. Later, Washington city was burned in retaliation for this town and the burning of the capital buildings at York.

The American fleet returned to its base at Sackets Harbor, New York—totally victorious and with immense naval stores now available for their own ship building.

General Winfield Scott

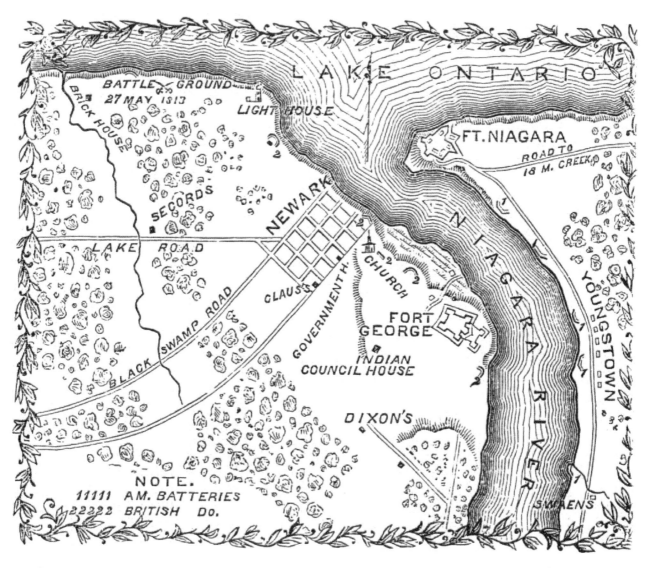

Fort George   Courtesy of Bernard J. Lossing

Visit the battlefield: http://www.pc.gc.ca/eng/lhn-nhs/on/fortgeorge/index.aspx

Chapter 8:
The Defense of Sackets Harbor

In the months following incursion by the British, the tiny lake port of Sackets Harbor, in upstate New York, developed into the largest American Great Lakes base. With its strategic position, superb natural harbor and abundant resources, it was destined to become the center of military and naval operations for the northern theatre of the war. But it would not become so without a good deal of courage and sacrifice.

After eight years of mortal combat, England finally defeated Napoleon. This freed up British troops for the invasion of the United States. The Earl of Bathhurst, British Secretary of Colonial Affairs, issued the following secret order to Governor General George Prevost, calling not only for the containment and dismemberment of the U.S., but also for the complete destruction of the Sackets naval base:

From Earl Bathhurst, 3rd June 1814

Reinforcements allotted for North America and the operations contemplated for the employment of them.

SECRET
Downing Street
3rd June 1814

Sir,
    I have already communicated to you in my dispatch of the 14th of April the intention of His Majesty's government to avail themselves of the favorable state of affairs in Europe, in order to reinforce the Army under your Command. I have now to acquaint you with the arrangements which have been made in consequence, and to point out to you the views with which His Majesty's Government have made is considerable an augmentation of the Army in Canada.
    The 2nd Battalion of the Royal Scots of the strength stated in the margin (768) sailed from Spithead on the 9th ulto. direct for Quebec, and was joined at Cork by the 97th Regiment destined to relieve the Nova Scotia Fencibles at Newfoundland; which latter will immediately proceed to Quebec.
    The 6th and 82nd Regiments of the strength (980, 837) sailed from Bordeaux on the 15th ulto. direct for Quebec.
    Orders have also been given for embarking at the same port twelve of the most effective Regiments of the Army under the Duke of Wellington together with the three companies of Artillery on the same service. This Force, which/when joined by the detachments about to proceed from this country will not fall short of 10,000 Infantry, will proceed in three divisions to Quebec. The first of these divisions will embark immediately, the second a week after the first and the third as soon as the means of transport are collected. The last division however will arrive in Quebec long before the close of the year.

Six other Regiments have also been detached from the Gironde and the Mediterranean four of which are destined to be employed in a direct operation against the Enemy's Coast, and the other two are intended as a reinforcement to Nova Scotia and New Brunswick, available / if circumstances appear to you to render it necessary / for the defense of Canada, or for the offensive operations on the Frontier to which your attention will be particularly directed. It is also in contemplation at a later period of the year to make a more serious attack on some part of the Coast of the United States, and with this view a considerable force will be collected at Cork without delay (New Orleans?*). These operations will not fail to effect a powerful diversion in your favor.

The result of this arrangement as far as you are immediately concerned will be to place at your disposal the Royals, The Nova Scotia Fencibles, the 6th and the 82nd Regiments amounting to 3,127 men; and to afford you in the course of the year a further reinforcement of 10,000 British troops.

When this force shall have been placed under your command His Majesty's Government conceive that the Canada's will not only be protected for the time against any attack which the Enemy may have the means of making, but it will enable you to commence offensive operations on the Enemy's Frontier before the close of this campaign. At the same time it is by no means the intention of His Majesty's Government to encourage such forward movements into the Interior of the American territory as might commit the safety of the force placed under your Command. The object of your operations will be, first, to give immediate protection. Secondly, to obtain if possible ultimate security to His Majesty's possessions in America. The entire destruction of Sackets Harbor and the Naval Establishment on Lake Erie and Lake Champlain come under the first description. The maintenance of Fort Niagara and so much of the adjacent Territory as may be deemed necessary, and the occupation of Detroit and the Michigan Country came under the second. Your successes shall enable us to terminate the war by the retention of the Fort of Niagara, and the restoration of Detroit and the whole of the Michigan Territory to the Indians. The British frontier will be materially improved. Should there be any advance position on that part of our frontier which extends towards Lake Champlain, the occupation of which would materially tend to the security of the province, you will if you deem it expedient expel the Enemy from it, and occupy it by detachments of the Troops under your command, Always however, taking care not expose his Majesty's Forces to being cut off by too extended a line of advance.

If you should not consider it necessary to call to your assistance the two regiments which are to proceed in the first instance to Halifax, Sir J. Sherbrooke will receive instruction to occupy as much of the District of Maine as will secure an uninterrupted intercourse between Halifax and Quebec.

In contemplation of the increased force which by this arrangement you will be under the necessity of maintaining in the Province directions have been given for shipping immediately for Quebec provisions for 10,000 men for 6 months.

The Frigate which conveys this letter has also on board 100,000 pounds in specie for the use of the Army under your command. An equal sum will also be embarked on board the Ship of War which my be appointed to convoy to Quebec the fleet which is expected to sail from this country on the 10th or at latest on the 15th instant.

I have the honor to be
Sir
Your most obedient
Humble Servant
BATHURST"

The above secret order was found among the private family papers of Sir Christopher Prevost, 6th Baronet, at his home in Albufeira, Portugal. The order remained secret into the next century. It was discovered at the British Public Records Office in 1922 but lost again soon after. This copy of the order, Sir George's, was unearthed with the help of Sir Christopher. Boldface is author's emphasis. *Author's note.

Prevost also wanted Maine, New Hampshire and Vermont for a winter land route to British Canada, avoiding the frozen St. Lawrence River. He knew that this new country would rival England's economic power and that whoever controlled the Great Lakes would have possession of Canada. Lopping off the Northeastern states of the U.S. would be a multiple triumph.

Marine Captain Richard Smith had been sent to Sackets Harbor with 100 Marines to guard the yard and naval stores. A naval shipyard surrounding the harbor engaged as many as 3,000 sailors and workmen in what became the first naval arms race in North America. Eventually, almost half of the USMC, 300 Marines, were stationed at Sackets. At this point, Sackets' "boom-town" nature had caused it to become a dirty, sickly place with waste thrown into the streets. Eight to ten soldiers died of sickness daily and, of the 175 Marines present at this battle, only 30 were fit for combat. Also, Sackets was remote from the highways of American manufacturing—the heavy gear such as hawsers, anchors and great guns (24- and 32-pounders) were brought in by batteaux from New York City via the Mohawk River and Oswego—and it was insecure against weather or hostilities. Similarly, the British naval base at Kingston, Ontario, 35 miles due north on Lake Ontario, had to deal with long supply lines reaching all the way to England itself. A frenzy of shipbuilding ensued on both sides—each side making a larger ship than the enemy's latest endeavor.

Sackets was to be held at all costs. Commodore Chauncey of the Great Lakes fleet, along with Gen. Macomb, fortified the base in depth. From west to east was the Basswood Cantonment, constructed primarily from basswood, which housed the American regulars: the 9th, 21st, and 23rd U.S. Infantry, the Light 3rd Artillery and the 1st Light Dragoons. Because of the intense cold and wind from Lake Ontario (the snow could reach as deep as eight feet), these troops had the luxury of permanent wood barracks instead of canvas tents. Next was Fort Tompkins with its massive 32-pounder cannon on a six-foot-high, raised swivel. The great gun was manned by experienced cannoneers.

Behind this were the Marine barracks, featuring another rare luxury—fireplaces. The Marines were to fight from these barracks through walls pierced with loopholes for firing. They would be held in reserve until the initial combat at the fort required them to engage in the hottest part of the fight. Next were three gun batteries trained to protect the Navy yard and its around-the-clock ship building.

South of the harbor was Fort Volunteer—the last defense. Macomb had done a splendid job here, creating an impregnable mobile defense in depth just like they did at the battles of Cowpens and Guilford Courthouse during the Revolutionary War. The hospital and the town were just south of the yard. It and the defensive works were ringed with abatis (felled, sharpened trees—the barbed wire of its day). This ring funneled the advancing British right into the killing ground of Fort Tompkins and that deadly swivel.

A total of 5,200 American regulars, dragoons and Marines would be in the fight, not counting the sailors. They were supported by 700 local militia from Jefferson County and the Albany Volunteers. The militia was considered unreliable and usually fled after firing a couple of volleys. All American troops were instructed to load their muskets with a .75 caliber round ball and 3 buckshots. This quadrupled their firepower compared to the British single shot. Both sides were also told to fire at the enemy's officers.

General Prevost learned through spies that Chauncey was out with the fleet burning York and obliterating Fort George. This would be the perfect opportunity to attack Sackets. The British fleet, sailing from Kingston and commanded by Commodore Yeo, attacked at 3:30 a.m. of May 29, 1813. They towed 50 batteaux and war canoes filled with companies from the 1st, 8th, 100th , and 104th of Foot plus the Gengarries, Voltigeurs (French Canadians from Quebec), and a party of Mohawk and Mississauges. These attackers totaled 1,570 men.

The British thought they were going against weak militia because they'd captured all of Aspinwall's 175 reinforcements before they landed. With no wind, the British sat in their boats for a whole day as American reinforcements poured into Sackets from all over New York. The troops answered the call just as they'd done against Burgoyne at Saratoga, 36 years earlier.

The British force landed at the north side of Horse Island to form up and easily pushed off the American militia. The American pivot gun opened up on their 33 troop-laden batteaux and columns to devastating effect. The British then marched onto the causeway that connected the mainland. Marching eastward, the British had the rising sun in their eyes and could not see the disposition of the formidable American works. Unfortunately for their fleet, the lake was glass-smooth with no wind, which prevented them from getting close enough to bombard the yard and the village. They eventually had to recourse to using "sweeps" (rowing the ship through oars inserted in the cannon ports) and "hedging" (dropping the anchor way in front of the ship and then winding it to pull the ship forward) to get their ships in closer. Gen. Macomb's abatis fortifications ringing the base forced the British infantry to take the lake road heading toward the heavily fortified Fort Tompkins. Its lone 32-pounder cannon on a pivot, firing solid shot and grape, was devastating to British boats and infantry in column.

Blinded by white smoke, the Voltigeurs fired a volley into the backs of the 100th of Foot who were formed up right in front of them. After a few volleys from the American militia (who promptly fled), the British met the American infantry formed outside the palisades of Fort Tompkins. After murderous fire, the British were winning the battle and more American militia were retreating on the Adams Center Road. The fighting became very intense with hand-to-hand combat and the British firing into the Marine loopholes—men firing directly into each others' faces. The British were especially strong in this fight as the poor common soldier had visions of great wealth to be acquired by plundering the town.

British Major Drummond, a fearless leader, was knocked down by an American sniper. His men had implored him to take off his gold epaulettes before the battle, so the bullet struck the metal epaulettes in his pocket, resulting in only a nasty bruise instead of a mortal wound. In fact, every British officer received a wound of some kind during this intense four-hour battle.

Eventually, the British got around to the north side of the fort where Chauncey's son gave the signal for the munitions and yard to be burned. Later, recriminations would abound as to who actually gave the order. Marine Sergeant Solomon Fisher had been told to have a bonfire ready by the upper barracks as a signal to fire the buildings containing ships' fittings and the stores captured at York. The Marines were assigned the mission of burning the ship *General Pike* which was under construction, along with all naval stores, including the Marine barracks, to prevent their capture in case the harbor was taken. When the orders were finally countermanded, the Marines were able to extinguish the fire on the *General Pike,* thanks to its green wood, but the Marine barracks and storehouse were already ablaze and Capt. Smith's Marines lost everything. It took months to replace sails and stores to complete the ships. The Americans had mistakenly done what the British failed to do.

However, Prevost, a civilian Governor-General and not a military man, was by nature overly cautious in his command. When his ships could not land cannon, he gave up all hope of overwhelming Fort Thompkins. Only one ship, the *Beresford*, came up to engage and its effort was minimal due to American counter-fire. Prevost called for a parley in the middle of the battle. When the Americans would not surrender, the British simply left and the Americans did not pursue. In amazement, the Americans watched as the British returned to their boats and quit the battle. Their march turned into a rout and they left their wounded and dead behind along the lake road on which they had advanced.

The British lost 25 percent of their men: 50 killed and 211 wounded. The Americans lost 47 killed, 84 wounded and 36 missing. Lieutenant Colonel Aspinwall's 9th U.S. Infantry from Massachusetts accounted for most of the casualties—the 9th had fought as hard as their fathers had at Bunker Hill. Private Francis Lawrence, a bounty jumper from Montreal, deserted from the Marines and re-enlisted in the 21st U.S. Infantry for the extra bounty. After the battle, the unforgiving Marine Corps caught up with him and he was shot. USMC Private Elisha Johnson was also shot as a deserter. In addition, 150 Americans were captured at the beginning of the battle when a regimental reinforcement was approaching the harbor during the British landing.

Sackets was one of the toughest running fights of the war. The attack did slow the American ship-building effort and relegated the planned U.S. invasion of lower Canada to failure. But ultimately, the British lost much more than they had gained. Again, Marine musketry had proved invaluable in the fight.

If the British had been victorious at Sackets Harbor, they would have gone on to Lake Erie and burned Perry's fleet being built at Presque Isle at Erie, Pennsylvania, and that loss would have subsequently cost the Americans three territories—Michigan, Indiana and Illinois. During the remainder of the war, Sackets was never attacked again. It was reinforced a third time with additional troops, three

Marine sentry guarding timber supply column for U.S. shipbuilding
Artist: Colonel Charles H. Waterhouse, USMCR

more forts and two additional batteries. Eleven vessels ultimately were built there, making up the majority of the Lake Ontario fleet including the 110-gun behemoth *New Orleans.* Unusual as it might sound, the ships' cannon and anchors were removed and the ships were sunk in the harbor during the winter for cold storage, then raised in the spring. Sackets Harbor represented the largest American military shipbuilding effort and the largest Marine base in one locale up to that time. It was the first planned army installation in American military history.

The Defense of Sackets Harbor   Courtesy of Jim Parker

Visit the battlefield: http://www.sacketsharborbattlefield.org

Chapter 9: The Battle of Craney Island

As the War of 1812 progressed, the British raided several Eastern seaboard towns. On June 22, they turned their sights on the Norfolk navy yard where the Americans were building faster, better frigates. A destroyed Norfolk would help the British ensure their mastery of the seas.

Craney Island was 30 acres standing at the approach to the city at Hampton Roads. It was fortified with two 24-pounders, one 18-pounder, and four 6-pounders, all on the southeast side of the island. Brigadier General Robert Taylor, commanding officer of the district, had two companies of artillery from Portsmouth under Major Faulkner of the Virginia State Artillery. Also included were a company of rifleman under Captain Roberts and 416 militia infantry under Lieutenant Colonel Beatty. These Americans had no means of escape if overrun, but they were "all cool and collected, rather wishing for the attack."

General Taylor, seeing the U.S. force assembled, called for more men. Thirty regulars under Captain Pollard from Fort Norfolk, 30 volunteers under Lieutenant Johnson of Culpepper plus 150 seamen and 50 Marines under Marine Lieutenant Breckinridge were sent specifically to work the heavy guns. The American force, well aware of British intentions, now had 737 men situated where the British were expected.

At midnight, the American camp was alarmed by the crack of sentry Private Shutte's musket. He had thought he heard a boat in the straights. The troops were called to arms and stood until dawn, but only a lone bush was seen floating towards the battery. No sooner had they stood down when a horseman dashed in and reported the British were landing two miles to the west at Major Hoffleur's place.

Drums beat the long roll and, as daylight appeared, the British anchored in the Roads were seen moving in boats from their ships to the shore. Maj. Faulkner, a cool and skilled artillerist, ordered the three heavy guns on the southeast end of the island repositioned to the northwest next to the four 6-pounders commanded by Marine Lieutenant (later Major) Hale who was lying in wait. The merchantman *Manhattan* transferred the guns from one end of the island to the other. These seven guns in battery made a formidable defense. The infantry, riflemen and extra artillerymen formed a line behind the guns facing the strait at the mouth of Wise's creek.

The 18-pounder was manned by the sailors and Marines from the U.S. Frigate *Constellation*. The two 24-pounders and the 6-pounders were officered by Capt. Emerson and commanded by Lt. Col. Beatty. A long pole was made and the U.S. flag was nailed to it and placed in the redoubt. A crescent of U.S. gunboats was stationed in a line stretching from Craney Island to Lambert's Point. The *Constellation* lay nearer to the city of Norfolk.

The British landed 2,500 infantry and Royal Marines at Hoffleur's Creek. They stealthily crept through the forest and emerged at the confluence of Wise's Creek and the strait. They opened up with a barrage from a field-piece, a howitzer and a bevy of Congrieve rockets to cover the movement of a detachment that had been sent to cross the creek and gain the rear of the Americans' left flank. The Americans answered with grape and canister and drove the flank attack out of reach of the artillery.

At the same time, British land barges approached with 1,500 sailors and Royal Marines that had been offloaded from their ships. They hugged the shore in two parallel lines to keep out of range of the gunboat artillery. They were led by Admiral Warren's beautiful barge, the twenty-four-oar *Centipede*, which had a brass 3-pounder (called a Grasshopper) in the bow and was painted a rich green. She was commanded by Captain Hanchett, a natural son of King George III.

The Americans waited anxiously as the onslaught slowly approached. Faulkner gave a signal to Emerson who shouted, "Now my brave boys, are you ready?"

"All ready," was the reply.

"Fire!" exclaimed Faulkner. The whole battery erupted with round, grape and canister shot blasting into the enemy. The volleys formed a storm of metal but the British kept coming until it was too terrible to endure. Their barges were thrown into disarray. The *Centipede* was hulled by a diagonal shot wounding several men including the leg of Capt. Hanchett. Orders were given to retreat and the flotilla turned back to their ships. The *Centipede* and four other barges were sunk in shoal water but Lieutenant Neale and some bold seamen waded in and captured the admiral's barge. Among the cutlasses, small cannon, and pistols in its bow was found a little terrier. The *Centipede* was later used as a U.S. guard boat.

The British had thought this fight would be a cakewalk and had brought their breakfast, shaving kits and dogs with them but before sunset, the attack on Norfolk, the *Constellation* and the navy yard was abandoned. The battle had ended with no American losses. The British lost six killed, 24 wounded and 114 missing. Of the latter, 40 were prisoners and deserters.

Frustrated by their repulse, the British went on to attack the village of Hampton, Virginia. They burned the town and a company of Chasseurs—composed of French turncoats—raped a number of American women. The British, embarrassed by their action, shipped the Chasseurs off to Halifax, Nova Scotia.

Craney Island was the first U.S. Marine battle where a detachment repulsed a battalion of Royal Marines back into the sea. The Marines' excellent training in working the great guns had saved the Norfolk naval yard—resulting in a stunning and strategically important victory for America.

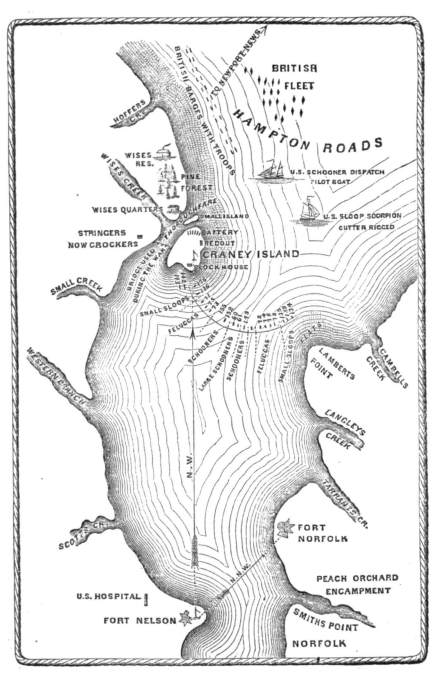

Courtesy of Bernard J. Lossing

Visit the battlefield:
http://www.norfolkhistorical.org/fort/index.html

Chapter 10:
The Attempt to Retake Mackinac Island

Twenty-nine days after war was declared on July 17, 1812, Mackinac Island was captured by the British. The Island was the crossroads of the North Country and the American fur industry depended on it. The Americans were very determined to get it back.

Pressured by American fur mogul and naval sponsor John Jacob Astor, the Secretary of the Navy commanded Commodore Isaac Chauncey to order Commodore Perry to retake Mackinac and St. Joseph Island. Flush with two great American victories at the Battle of Lake Erie and The Thames, Perry's squadron set sail on June 20, 1814. Lieutenant Colonel George Croghan commanded the 2nd Regt. of Riflemen and the flotilla and its Marines were commanded by Commodore Arthur Sinclair.

After three raids on the way to the island, the American officers were stymied as to how to take the awesome British Fort Mackinac situated on a 250-foot limestone cliff. Because of this height, Sinclair knew his ship's cannon were useless against the fort. The Americans decided to attack the fort from the northwest side of the island, the same landing place the British had used two years earlier. They would have to fight their way through two miles of heavy, Indian-infested woods.

The British, knowing an attack was imminent, had recently reinforced the fort with two companies of the experienced Royal Newfoundland Fencibles and a small detachment of the Royal Regt. of Artillery consisting of one 6-pounder and one 3-pounder cannon. With Lewis Crawford's 50 militia and 350 Indians, the British totaled 550 men.

On the morning of August 4, five American vessels anchored 300 yards offshore on the northwest side of the island and opened up with a tremendous barrage to sweep the landing place. Five companies (500 men) of American regiments, detached from the 17th, 19th, and 24th Regiments of Infantry, hit the beach first. Colonel William Cotgreave led 250 Ohio Volunteer Militia and a detachment of the Corps of Artillery bringing up several 6-pounder cannon. Marine Lt. Hyde led his detachment of Marines ashore to serve as a reserve.

After the bombardment, the American force of 850 men set out on a narrow track through the woods towards Dousman's farm. Both the Americans and the British had chosen to fortify the farm since it was the only clearing in the heavy woods and underbrush. As it was, the clearing was only about 500 yards square. British commander Lieutenant Colonel Robert McDouall fortified the southern end of the clearing with abatis of fallen trees. His plan was to fire a volley and then follow with a bayonet charge against the American line. The Indians on both flanks were positioned so the Americans couldn't outflank the redcoats.

As soon as Croghan's men reached the north end of the field, they came under artillery fire from the two British cannon. The Americans started to advance but soon realized that advancing on the open field under rapid canister shot would be suicidal. They began encircling on both flanks with the main thrust on the left. Suddenly a band of Menominee Indians—led by chiefs Tomah, Yellow Dog and L'Espagnol—opened fire on the American column, killing Maj. Holmes, severely wounding Capt. Robert Desha and downing a number of his troops.

The Americans panicked, thinking they were surrounded in the heavy woods. They retreated to their main position, then moved forward again towards the center of the British line—but the fight had gone out of them. A retreat was ordered back to the cover of the ships' guns and the Marines acted as the rear guard. Only one Marine, Sergeant James Tull, was wounded.

The Americans lost Maj. Holmes and ten privates killed while three officers and 50 men were wounded. Two more privates were missing and Capt. Isaac Van Horne, Jr., Lt. Hezekiah Jackson, and four enlisted men would later die of their wounds. Under a flag of truce, the body of Maj. Holmes was recovered and returned to Detroit for burial. The enlisted men's remains, though severely mutilated by the Indians, were buried on the battlefield. The most serious loss to the British was Wee-kah, a Menominee chief.

The American fleet withdrew to Thunder Bay where a squadron set out for Nottawasaga Bay where they destroyed a small British supply base along with the British schooner *Nancy*.

Mackinac post would be held by the British until July, 1815, when by the Treaty of Ghent, it was returned along with the Michigan Territory—including northern Michigan and Wisconsin—to the United States.

Fort Mackinac   Artist: Seth Eastman

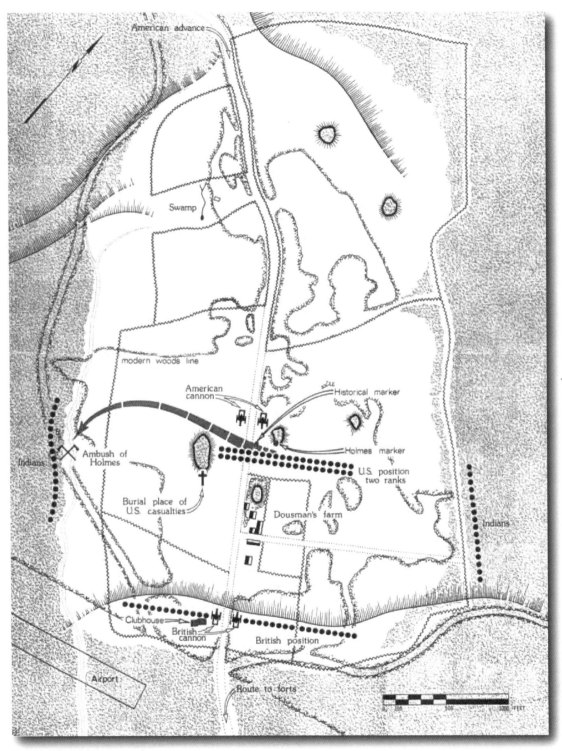

Courtesy of Mackinac State Parks

Visit the battlefield: http://www.mackinacparks.com/fort-mackinac/

Chapter 11: The Battle of Lake Erie

With the fall of three American forts—Chicago, Detroit and Mackinac—in the summer of 1812, President Madison and his war council decided that military supremacy on the Great Lakes, especially on Lakes Ontario and Erie, was paramount in order to stem the British onslaught. If British domination over the lakes could be stopped by capturing Montreal and all of Lower Canada (Quebec), then supplies, war material and troops would not be able to reach the Western frontier—and British incursions would cease.

The American base at Sackets Harbor in upstate New York on Lake Ontario was picked to become the main base for American operations. A large naval and Marine installation was hurriedly built, several forts erected, and preparations were made to attack the British fleet at Kingston, 35 miles due North.

The dilemma for the American commander, Commodore Chauncey, was how to fight on two lakes separated by Niagara Falls when his two fleets were only now being built. There were few officers and shipbuilders available and not enough sailors and Marines to form detachments on all ships. He determined that the Lake Ontario fleet would have priority because the main British harbor was also engaged in a ship-building arms race. The Lake Erie squadron under Commodore Perry and Marine Lieutenant John Brooks would have to wait for their crews and Marines until after Sackets Harbor was first supplied and secured. After all, the Corps had just been re-formed in 1798, and there were only about 1,200 officers and men to go around.

Lieutenant John Brooks was the son of Governor Brooks of Massachusetts. He was considered a firebrand and a good officer, though he'd been shipped west to cool off from a potential duel with another Marine officer over gambling. Brooks brought 18 Marines with him from the Washington Navy Yard. Hundreds more Marines had been expected from Commodore Chauncey but as it turned out, Gen. Harrison's army (especially the 137th and 147th Pennsylvania regiments) were levied to fight as Marines. These frontiersmen were expert marksmen with their Pennsylvania rifles and would add devastating firepower to the Marine detachment. The British soldier feared the American long rifle and called it "the best widow maker in North America."

Brooks' plan for the nine American ships was to have full Marine units on the two brigs—the *Lawrence* and the *Niagara*—and Marine NCOs on the other ships, directing the militia marksmen. Normally each ship would have 50 Marines on board including an officer, a fifer and a drummer, providing firepower during battles. They would fight as six-man squads on the "tops" (platforms on the mast) with one marksman firing and five loading and passing the loaded rifle forward. They were also trained to replace cannon crews that were disabled and to lead boarding and landing parties. They acted as ship's guards as well—sleeping between the ship's officers and the crew to deter mutiny.

But Brooks would have to make do with only his 18 Marines. These men were equipped with a .75 caliber sea-service musket. The captured arm was a 3rd India-pattern British "Brown Bess" musket, shortened for easier loading among the rigging. A Marine was expected to load, ram and fire three rounds a minute and, unlike the British, they kept their eyes open on firing. They also carried a 16-inch bayonet and a battle-ax, as well as grenades that would be thrown from the tops at the enemy and at open British magazine hatches. Quite a few ships were blown sky high by a well-lobbed grenade.

The saws, axes, and hammers clanging on the forges produced the lake fleet in record time. Cannons cast in Pittsburgh, 120 miles south of Erie, Pennsylvania—Perry's base—were carried overland by sledges. When finished, Perry's fleet boasted 54 guns able to throw 900 pounds of iron per broadside against the enemy. The *Lawrence* and the brig *Niagara* each had 20 cannon; the *Caledonia*, three; the schooner *Ariel*, four; *Scorpion*, two; *Somers*, two; sloop *Tripe*, one; and *Porcupine*, one. Most of these cannon were newly invented carronades or "smashers" which were devastating, though only at close range. Even in these early days, America's success in battle was partly due to having the most advanced technology.

The Americans positioned their ships at Put-in Bay, Ohio—ideally situated to intercept any traffic between Malden and Long Point, Ontario, which was fast becoming a British stronghold.

When the British fleet from Malden appeared northwest of Put-in Bay, they had the *Detroit* with 19 guns; *Queen Charlotte*, 17; *Lady Prevost*, 13; the brig *Hunter*, ten; the sloop *Little Belt*, three; and the schooner *Chippewa*, one—for a total of 63 guns and 460 pounds of iron broadside, but very few carronades. Their crews and provincial marines had been hastily assembled and had no gunnery practice, whereas the American gun crews were experienced. Some of the Americans had fought on the *Constitution* and others were from ships out of Newport, Rhode Island.

When the two fleets closed for battle on Sept. 10, 1812, every American ship in line knew exactly the ship they were to attack. The British battle line also had a precise strategy. The British pounced on the *Lawrence* first since they wanted to destroy the largest ship. This was where Lt. Brooks and most of the Marines were stationed. Three ships—the *Detroit*, *Queen Charlotte* and *Hunter*—formed a crescent around the *Lawrence* with the *Hunter* getting behind the *Lawrence*. They proceeded to rake her—firing broadside across the length of the ship, smashing everything in its path. The carnage was immense.

Lieutenant Brooks, commander of the Marine detachment, was standing next to Perry when Brooks was hit by a 32-pounder cannonball taking away his hip. He was hurled across the deck and asked Perry to kill him, for the pain was excruciating. Perry refused and ordered the Marines to carry him below. The Lieutenant held on for some time, dying only after he learned the outcome of the battle. Others met the same fate. Perry attracted so much fire it seemed that anyone standing next to him was doomed.

The *Lawrence* was a wreck in two hours. Perry asked the surgeon for walking wounded to work the guns—whose crews were already mangled. The cockpit where the wounded were served was above the waterline, allowing broadsides to wreak even more havoc on the already-wounded. Pohig, a Narragansett Indian, was first wounded in the arm and then had both of his legs taken off by a cannonball. Eventually, only one gun was left, and Perry helped aim her.

The brig *Niagara*, captained by Lt. Elliot, had been lagging behind, untouched. Elliott had an attitude problem because he'd been passed over for command and now, meeting Perry in the heat of battle, all he would say was, "How goes the day?" Perry curtly ordered him to bring the other American ships up fast. Finally, the *Niagara* came to relieve the *Lawrence* and Perry immediately transferred his battle flag, "Don't give up the ship," via a jolly boat to the *Niagara*.

It was an incredibly brave move and the American crews cheered wildly. Of course, every British ship poured fire on the *Lawrence*'s jolly boat—round shot, grape, cannister of one-inch musket balls, and musket shot. Perry's little boat was hit by a cannon ball and he plugged the hole with his coat. Finally, Perry ordered the *Lawrence* to haul down her colors to ease the killing of his men. The smaller American craft now closed in on the British.

The *Niagara*, fresh with full cannons and Marines, then broke the British line and fired at two ships on larboard and three on starboard. The *Detroit* and the *Queen Charlotte* got their bowsprits tangled and the American ships raked them unmercifully. One broadside from the *Niagara* literally tore the *Lady Prevost* to pieces. Aboard that ship, British Lieutenant Buchan suffered a shot in the face from an American Marine. Perry ordered the Marines to cease fire on the *Lady Prevost* as her resistance was over.

Meanwhile, the Marine marksmen poured volleys and grenades at the British. The battle was a horrific cacophony of ear-shattering broadsides, crashing timber, tearing canvas and the screams of dying men.

The *Niagara*'s bold example brought all the American ships into the heat of the battle. In just eight minutes, four British ships surrendered and two tried to flee but were overtaken. Victory was complete. This was the first time in history that an entire British squadron was captured—and by an infant 30-year old country at that. So frightening was the battle that a number of Canadian Indians were found hidden and skulking for safety aboard the English vessels. They had been engaged as marksmen but the first shot had taken all the fight out of them.

Perry fired off a letter to the Secretary of the Navy: "Sir—it has pleased the Almighty to give into the arms of the United States a signal victory over their enemies on this lake. The British squadron, consisting of two ships, two brigs, one schooner and one sloop, have this moment surrendered to the force under my command after a sharp conflict. I have the honor to be, sir, very respectfully, your obedient servant, Oliver Hazard Perry."

The Americans had 123 casualties, 27 of whom were killed. The British counted 135, 41 of whom died. Perry, on returning to the *Lawrence* told Purser Hambleton, "The prayers of my wife have prevailed in saving me." He had accepted the British surrender from nine defeated officers on the blood strewn deck of the *Lawrence*. Sick all this time with fever, Perry lay down and slept among the dead for hours.

On the following day, they buried the dead at sea and all 15 ships shoved off to Put-in-Bay. After repairs, six dead officers including Lt. Brooks, USMC, were buried on South Bass Island. The Perry Victory Monument enshrines them today and Congress posthumously awarded Lt. Brooks a silver medal. He was the first Marine in history to receive a Congressional medal.

The six British ships were sold for $242,250. That prize money was divided by 596 officers, seamen and Marines in proportion to their rank. Perry received $7,140, a fortune at that time, and the average Marine received $214.59. The slain men's shares were given to their parents.

The 300 captured British officers and seamen, plus 14 officer's wives and 28 children, were transported to Camp Bull in Chillicothe, then capital of Ohio. They were soon joined by 601 captured British infantry and several Indians from the battle of the Thames. The British officers were allowed to retain their servants and the men lived in fine style, attending many town functions including observing the execution of six American deserters. The following year they were all exchanged and paroled.

The battle of Lake Erie was a much needed victory for the United States. It showed that the Americans could take on the powerful British navy. And it gave General Harrison and his Army of the Northwest a clear path to Upper Canada (today's Ontario), enabling his subsequent victory over the British and Indians at the battle of the Thames. Indian leader Tecumseh was killed at Thames and the Indian coalition was broken.

The victory at Erie ultimately kept the Michigan, Indiana and Illinois Territories—originally intended by the British to be an Indian state—in the union. Once again a mere handful of Marines, through their courage and fighting skills, had made an outstanding contribution to the future of our country.

Battle of Lake Erie　　　　　　　　Artist: William Henry Powell

The Niagara Breaks the English Line   From a painting by Carlton T. Chapman

Directions to Perry's Victory & International Peace Memorial:
http://www.nps.gov/pevi/index.htm

Chapter 12: Heroic Stand at Bladensburg

By June of 1814, the British had been blockading the American coast for 18 months. With 4,000 regulars, Royal Marines, and negroes bribed with promises of freedom, they were also poised to invade Washington. The British commander, Vice Admiral Cochrane, was being urged by Sir George Prevost, Governor General of Canada, to burn the city in retaliation for the Americans' burning of Canadian Parliament buildings in York and for the burning of Newark.

The Navy ordered Commandant Wharton to raise a battalion of Marines to help protect the Chesapeake Bay from incursion; President Madison assigned Brigadier General Winder to lead a composite force of infantry, state militia and volunteer riflemen to defend Washington and; Commandant Joshua Barney, a tough, 54-year-old Revolutionary War veteran was assigned to the naval defense.

In June, Barney found himself still blockaded after a number of skirmishes with the 21-ship British fleet up the Patuxent River. The Marines under Captain Sam Miller had cooperated with Barney, supplying artillery fire from the shore, but he was unable to break through.

The British entered the Patuxent River on August 17, and two days later landed unopposed at Benedict, Maryland. Barney, outflanked and outmaneuvered by 40 British barges, had blown up his flotilla of 13 gun barges. The British started their 40-mile march to Washington.

Barney and his flotilla men joined Winder's men. Capt. Miller, with 110 Marines from the Washington Navy Yard, along with five artillery pieces, also joined them. The Marines now had two 18-pounders and three 12-pounders.

On Wednesday the 24th, the British approached Bladensburg four miles northeast of Washington at a bridge that crossed the eastern Potomac. Earlier, Gen. Winder had thought the British would attack Washington from the east in combination with their fleet passing Fort Washington south of the city.

Winder marched out of Washington and ordered Barney—much to Barney's disgust—to stay behind and guard the Eastern Branch Bridge (now the Sousa Bridge). At the bridge, Barney was able to personally complain to President Madison and had his orders changed. This was the only American battle where the President and his cabinet—the Attorney General, the Secretary of War, and Secretary of State—were all on the battlefield. The bridge was blown and Barney, his sailors, and Marines with their artillery, marched to the battle.

With the temperature at 100 degrees, the Americans were drawn up in three lines on the Washington side of the Potomac. The first line to encounter the advancing British were riflemen under Major Pinkney and two companies of militia under Captains Ducher and Gorsuch, and Captains Myers and Richard Magruder with 100 artillerymen and six 6-pounders from Baltimore.

The second line was composed of Bruch's artillery and Sterett's 1,350 men from the 5th Baltimore Volunteer Regiment under Lieutenant Colonels Ragan and Schutz.

The 3rd line—the heaviest—was made up of 1,200 men from a regiment of Maryland militia under Colonel Beall and 300 district militia from the 12th, 36th and 38th under Colonel Magruder (not to be confused with the junior officer, Captain Magruder from Baltimore). The center was held by Barney's flotilla men and the Marines' battery along with Scott and Peter's battery. Brent, with the 2nd Regt. of Smith's brigade and Waring's battalion of Maryland militia, were posted behind Peter's battery. A total of 7,000 men and 26 cannon were set to receive the British attack but of these, only 900 were enlisted men; the rest were untried militia.

Barney positioned his 500 flotilla men in the center, on a rise commanding the bridge and the road along which the British would come. On his right were 114 Marines and 370 sailors, all serving as infantry. Barney commanded the guns and Marine Captains Miller and Alex Sevier supervised the infantry.

The British crossed the bridge under heavy American fire and then retreated. They attacked again and took heavy casualties from American cannon. The American riflemen with their Pennsylvania rifles poured a deadly fire—but the British were continually being reinforced by more brigades joining the fray.

The Americans fell back to the 2nd line. The Yankees charged with the bayonet and once again pushed the British back. Then another British brigade came on line, turned the American left flank and started their rocket attack on the untrained militia. Ragan and Schutz' men were frightened by the rockets and fled. The 2nd line collapsed and now the British took on the 3rd line.

Barney's fire had a terrible effect on the redcoats. When the British moved to hit their right flank, they met Miller's Marine fire from the 12-pounders. The U.S. Marines were well trained in handling the great guns and wreaked havoc upon the enemy. The British were cut up, losing several officers including Colonel Thorton, who was severely wounded, and General Ross, who had his horse shot from under him. The Marines were obstinate and maintained their position against fearful odds.

Because they were heavily outnumbered, the Americans charged Navy-style. With the shout, "Repel boarders," the Marines attacked with bayonets and the Navy with cutlasses. The charge broke two British regiments, but the British light infantry took both of the Marines' flanks, wounding Barney severely and killing his horse. Miller was down, badly wounded in the arm and out of action. The British flanked wide, forded the river, cut through the militia and overran the Americans. The American militia had failed to stand their ground because of a rumor launched by the British that the negroes had risen up on the day of the battle to fight for their freedom—the additional worry that their homes and families were in danger being more than they could bear. The Navy flotilla men stood their ground, retired in order, and left their dead and wounded. Both Barney and Miller were captured. The battle was over in four hours, and Gen. Winder was forced to order a general retreat.

The American lines with their troop dispositions would almost certainly have been competent to roll back the invasion except for the interference of the President and his cabinet. James Monroe, the Secretary of State, was credited with the American defeat after he moved the 2nd line a quarter-mile to the rear against Gen. Winder's wishes. This movement caused the 1st line to be unsupported, and exposed the 2nd line to rocket fire. This fickle civilian interference with Army decisions was seen again in Vietnam 152 years later.

The defense of Washington was a shameful affair. It was the most serious defeat of American arms ever experienced. The army had broken and fled, but Barney's men and Marines, even though overrun, had held their ground to heroic glory. The Marines had eight killed and 14 wounded. Miller and Sevier were brevetted majors. The Americans lost 26 killed and 51 wounded. The British attackers lost 500 killed and wounded.

Word got out to the Washington city inhabitants that "the British were coming," and 8,500 citizens began a sudden and confused exodus. The government, the Army, and even the Commandant of the Marine Corps fled the city. The national records and Army records were put in linen bags and taken to Leesburg, Virginia. Commandant Wharton took Captain Crabb and the Marine Barracks guard to Frederick, Maryland. The Marines guarded the paymaster whose flight from Washington scandalized the Corps.

That evening, the British marched six miles into Washington. Reduced to a pillaging party of 200 torch bearers, they entered the city of 900 buildings like barbarians. Admiral Sir George Cochrane delighted in torching cities and thirsted for plunder but thought Washington would pay a ransom to save the city from destruction. Ross sent an agent to discuss the ransom, but no one was there to negotiate with him. So the torches were lit.

The British burned some private buildings: The *National Intelligencer*, an anti-British newspaper; a rope-walk; and a tavern among them. Any house that fired a shot at the column was destroyed, just as had been done by Napoleon in Moscow. Ross' horse was killed in one such attack. After two nights in Washington, the British burned most of the public buildings: the unfinished Capitol, the Library of Congress, the Treasury buildings, the Arsenal, the barracks for 3,000 troops, and the President's house. The *White House* got its title later when the blackened building was whitewashed to cover up the scorch marks. In all, a total of two million dollars worth of property had been destroyed. Only the Patent Office was spared. Also burned were national shipping stores and buildings at the Navy Yard totaling one million dollars.

The British enacted martial law over the Washingtonians who had to remain indoors from sunset to sunrise under pain of death. At the Navy Yard, the Americans hid a quantity of powder and shot in a well. One British soldier peeking in the well with a match blew the place up, along with an adjacent powder magazine, killing 12 British and wounding 30. The light of the fired city was seen 40 miles away in Baltimore.

Supposedly, the Marine Barracks at Eighth and I Street was spared by the British because of the heroic U.S. Marine stand at Bladensburg, though some historians dispute this account.

The British would have burned more of the city save for a tornado and lightning storm that actually killed British soldiers and drove them off to their ships. Many believed this was divine intervention. It did seem as though God wanted democracy to prevail.

Houses were unroofed and the enemy left they way they had come, through Bladensburg. They left their dead on the battlefield and gave 90 of their wounded to Barney's men for care. They embarked at Benedict and three days later attacked Alexandria, Virginia.

The British had no intention of holding Washington. Their reason for staying in the U.S. was to invade Louisiana and take possession of the Mississippi valley. England and Spain both intensely disapproved of the Louisiana Purchase by the U.S. From Napoleon—so when the British attacked New Orleans, a cadre of civil servants came along with the British army to rule over the coveted territory.

The Battle of Bladensburg left little to celebrate—but Dolly Madison, the First Lady, did manage to save some of America's national treasures, most notably George Washington's famous portrait. The heroic stand of the Marines and Navy had allowed precious time for the removal of American documents to safety, including the Declaration of Independence.

Engraved portrait of Commodore Joshua Barney
Artist: Alonzo Chappel
Collection of the author

The Final Stand at Bladensburg   Artist: Colonel Charles H. Waterhouse, USMCR

Visit the Battlefield: Fort Lincoln Cemetery, 3101 Bladensburg Rd., Brentwood MD 20722

Chapter 13:
Bombardment at the White House

On August 27, 1814, three days after the capture of Washington, D.C., a British squadron appeared before Fort Washington. It consisted of one frigate of 36 guns, one of 38 guns, two rocket ships, two bomb vessels, and one schooner. The American Captain Dyson either misunderstood General Winder's order to repel or was in mortal fear, for he blew up and abandoned the fort without firing a gun. There is little doubt that the British fleet could have been kept below by the proper employment of the fort's heavy cannon—but Dyson chose not to fight and for his conduct he was dismissed from the service.

The British squadron now had nothing to fear and sailed upriver, anchoring off Alexandria on the 28th. The following morning, the squadron positioned its ships into a bombardment formation 100 yards from the wharves and prepared to level the town. The able-bodied men and their heavy guns had been sent from the fort to defend the city but not more than 100 men were left.

When the British squadron arrived there was little means to oppose, so the city sent a delegation to Commodore Gordon to ask what terms he would ask to spare the town. He replied that all naval stores and ordnance—all the shipping and its furniture, merchandise of every description in the city, and "refreshments" of every kind—must immediately be given up to him. (There was a good reason for demanding furniture—the British naval captains were running a furniture business selling American cabinetry to other ship Captains.) In addition, he demanded that the vessels the Americans had scuttled be raised and delivered to the British. If all of this was done, the town and the citizens would be spared, except for the public works.

The British allowed only one hour for a response to these harsh and humiliating terms—not nearly enough time for the Americans to comply, even if they so chose. The merchandise that had already been carried from the town, as well as the sunken vessels, could not be given up.

So the British burned one vessel and loaded five captured ships and other craft with 16,000 pounds of flour, 150 bales of cotton, 1,000 hogsheads of tobacco and 5,000 dollars worth of wine and cigars. The squadron, now a fleet, weighed anchor and sailed down the Potomac.

Upon hearing of the surrender of Alexandria, the U.S. government determined to capture or destroy the British squadron on its descent of the Potomac. The Maryland and District militia could not be rallied in time, so the Secretary of the Navy sent an order to Commodore Rodgers in Baltimore to hurry with as large a number of Marines and sailors as he could assemble. Fifty Marines and 400 seamen, along with four 12-pounder cannon, were placed under the command of Commodores Rodgers, Perry, Porter and Creighton. Armed boats and fire-ships were prepared and these, along with the Marines and sailors—accompanied by the Virginia militia—were able to give the enemy a great deal of trouble.

Batteries were placed on the river bank at the White House, a short distance below Mount Vernon, and at Indian Head, Maryland. Both positions were commanding points on opposite sides of the river. Musketmen were placed on the wooded shores. Cannon were taken up by volunteers and quickly placed in battery. For five days, from September 1, they kept the British and their plundered vessels from descending the river. Meanwhile, the batteries and militia were supported by more cannon sent down from Washington and all the men that could be mustered from neighboring counties. The fighting became heavy.

The British employed a creative tactic. They were able to elevate their ships' guns by lowering the breeches and cutting away the gun ports so they could bear on the high bluffs. Finally their ten war vessels, with a total of 173 guns, brought such concentrated fire on Porter's battery at the White House and its supports, that it drove the Americans away. Perry's battery at Indian Head experienced a similar fate. His guns, managed by Lt. George Read, were also overwhelmed and the British were able to pass on to Chesapeake Bay.

Thus ended the British invasion which resulted in the capture of Washington, the destruction of its public buildings and Navy Yard, the surrender and plunder of Alexandria, and the profound humiliation of the American people. But in slowing the British advance down the Potomac, the Marines had demonstrated that their skills at the cannon could be instrumental in battle—and fortunately, better days were ahead.

Potomac River showing earthworks erected by David Porter against the
British squadron in September 1814

Capture of the City of Washington   Engraving dated 1815

Visit the Cannon Emplacements: Fort Belvoir, 9820 Flager Rd. Fort Belvoir, VA 22060

Chapter 14:
The Battle of Lake Champlain

The British defeat of Napoleon in April of 1814 freed up troops in Europe that the British could put to use in America. They planned to finalize the U.S. War of 1812 with a triple-pronged attack on three sides of the United States. The first two attacks were to be feints: first, an attack on New York state thru Lake Champlain; and second, raids on the Eastern seaboard resulting in the attacks on Fort McHenry and Baltimore and the burning of Washington, DC. The real objective was to be the capture of New Orleans, the second-largest American port, and subsequent control of the new Louisiana Territory. With its polyglot foreigners, the city was mistakenly thought to hold little allegiance to the U.S.

The Land Battle. The 15,000 British infantry, led by Sir George Prevost, Governor-General of Canada, were considered the finest infantry of the day. They were ordered to "destroy and lay waste" New York and they outnumbered the Americans four to one. The strategy was for the army to capture the three American forts manned by six infantry regiments in Plattsburgh, capture the state arsenal there, and then bombard the American fleet which would be trapped in a pincer movement between the army and the British naval squadron under Captain Downie. They prepared for the assault on the forts by making scaling ladders from horse racks found in local barns. They were to start the attack on land at the sound of the first broadside from the British Navy.

General Macomb, the American commander, had only 3,500 men remaining, 1,000 of whom were sick. Just a week earlier, Generald Izard had marched the other 4,000 men to Sackets Harbor where another British attack seemed eminent. Macomb knew he was outnumbered by Wellington's veterans so he decided to use hit-and-run tactics.

Colonel Appling's 100 riflemen started by felling trees in front of the enemy's advance and abatising the roads. Thousands of militia began pouring in from Vermont, New Hampshire and more New York counties, recalling how General Burgoyne's invasion had been stopped 39 years earlier. Groups of 100 to 300 men were sent to impede the British advance and fought three engagements. Captain Aiken's Company of Volunteer Riflemen, composed of 15 teenage marksmen, attacked a British column. Captain McGlissin, with 50 men, routed an entire 300-man rocket battery. Four large U.S. artillery batteries held up the British at two bridges whose planks were taken up and used for barricades. Hot shot (heated cannonballs, previously used only against ships) was fired into a part of the town to drive the British snipers out of the houses.

The British Army was getting across the Saranac River and had the upper hand when the American side suddenly sent up a loud cheer that the sea battle was won. This discouraged Gen. Prevost, who ordered an about face and headed back north, infuriating the British Army. A great quantity of munitions and provisions were abandoned as they retreated back to Montreal. Prevost felt that without the Navy's support, and with the American fleet on his flank, he could not sustain a deeper incursion into New York. He had proved to be a better governor than a General.

The Naval Battle. Commodore Thomas MacDonough, a firebrand, commanded the depleted American naval squadron. Earlier, two of his sloops were captured trying to slow the British advance down the Richelieu River, cutting his force by a third. MacDonough used the same tactic General Benedict

Arnold had used at the battle of Valcour Island 38 years earlier. He stationed his squadron on a north/south arc southwest of Cumberland point to await the British attack. In this way, he held the weather gauge—the wind in his favor—while the British had to beat into the wind to maneuver against the Americans.

The U.S. force consisted of four ships—the *Eagle, Saratoga, Ticonderoga*, and *Preble*, and ten gunboats, each carrying one or two cannons—for a total of 86 guns. They were manned by 882 sailors and Marines. The Marines performed a number of duties on board. They led all boarding parties and amphibious assaults. They fought on the tops—fighting platforms on the masts—as marksmen, and hurled grenades at the hatches where the powder magazines were stored. They were trained to man the great guns—24- or 32-pounder cannon—in case a cannon crew was taken out. They also provided discipline on board such as sleeping between the officers and crew to prevent mutiny. In this battle, about 200 infantry served as Marine sea soldiers providing musket fire.

The British also had four ships—the *Chub, Linnet, Confiance*, and *Finch*, along with ten galleys—for a total of 96 guns and more than a thousand men. Again, the Americans were outnumbered—but the U.S. troops had just learned of the burning of Washington and they were firmly resolved to win this fight.

Commodore MacDonough, a religious man, prayed with his officers before the battle. The American ships, formed in an arc, had their gunboats 40 yards behind them to prevent a rear maneuver. Their north flank was protected by Cumberland Point and to the south by shoals. The British had to come bow-in at them. This way, the American line could rake the enemy first, with the devastating broadside that swept the enemy's deck from bow to stern.

On the *Saratoga*, a gamecock's cage was struck by an opening cannonball. The rooster flew up into the rigging and squawked at the British which spirited the American gun crews. The battle was a horrific fight of ear-shattering broadsides, crashing timber, torn canvas and the screams of dying men. MacDonough's flagship, the *Saratoga*, caught on fire twice from hot shot. He waited for the British to close, because the Americans had 32-pound carronades or "smashers," which were the latest technology but were only effective at close range. MacDonough was knocked unconscious twice, once by a falling boom and again when the decapitated head of a gun crew captain hit him in the face.

The British worked the left and right flanks of the line as ships' cables were cut and drifted off. Lieutenant Cassin, U.S. Navy, while loading canister of 1-inch balls and bullet bags, had to repel British boarders again and again, but held the right of the line. The British were slaughtered. Their attacking galleys were so decimated that they could barely row away. Three British officers lay down on the deck, covered

Commodore Thomas MacDonough
Collection of the author

their ears and cowarded out. Every man on both sides was at the very least wounded.

The *Saratoga* and the *Eagle* now remained to slug it out with the *Confiance* and the *Linnet*. The quoins, or cannon elevating blocks, on the *Confiance* were not adjusted, causing its broadsides now to fire too high. Captain Downie of the *Confiance* was killed early by a flying timber. Some cannon were overloaded to the muzzle with shot, making them dangerous and ineffective.

The tactic that won the day for the Americans was MacDonough's use of "springs." These were lines that were pre-attached to anchors on the port side so they could not be shot away. When his ship was battered with over 55 hull hits, he came round with those lines to bring about the unused side of the ship to bear, with fresh cannon. The British tried the same maneuver but only came half-way round.

Captain MacDonough's victory message to Congress read: "The Almighty has been pleased to grant us a signal victory on Lake Champlain, in the capture of one frigate, one brig, and two sloops of war, of the enemy".

The battle cost the British 50 dead and 116 wounded. American casualties were 50 slain and 58 wounded. A Royal Marine who had fought with Admiral Nelson at Trafalgar said, "That battle was a flea bite compared to this fight." General Macomb, Commodore MacDonough and Lieutenant Cassin were awarded Congressional medals by Congress. Along with 119 other seaman, seven Marines still lie buried on Crab Island today in an unmarked grave. This battle was one of the most important engagements in American naval history. If it had been lost, the U.S. would have been short 33 states.

The above monument now stands on Crab Island, due to the author's efforts to honor the fallen sailors and Marines at this site. Courtesy of Ken Roberts.

The War of 1812 taught the U.S. three vital lessons for the future: First, the need for a standing army—never again would the country depend on county militias to fight experienced armies; second, that a series of coastal forts were needed—and built—to protect American port cities from Maine to Louisiana and; third, that there was a need for a bigger Navy with more frigates rather than small-craft gunboats expected to fight against Britain's 1,000 ships and 110-cannon men-of-war. Even the pacifists saw the need to end experimentation and listen to the professionals.

The Plight of the Confiance   Artist: Carlton T. Chapman

Visit the Battlefield: www.battleofplattsburgh.org

Chapter 15:
Marine Defense of Fort McHenry

After the burning of Washington, British General Ross wanted next to destroy Baltimore, America's nest for building swift "clipper-built" privateers. These ships and their crews had cost England over a million pounds in captured cargo. Baltimore was third in U.S. population at this time and was fourth in industry and wealth.

The city appropriated $20,000 for defense and began the job by fortifying the town with 40 cannon. From spring through fall, the city prepared their strong defense in full view of the British fleet, some of whose ships would intermittently raid Chesapeake villages. U.S. General Winder was put in command at Baltimore with 9,000 men. The U.S. Marines were placed in the center of the line to work the great guns.

The British, commanded by Gen. Ross and Admiral Cockburn, landed at North Point, 12 miles from the city. They numbered 9,000 men, including 2,000 Royal Marines. Unwilling to wait for their attack, the Americans marched out of their defenses to meet the enemy. Gen. Ross was killed by two teenage riflemen—Dan Wells and Henry McConas—who were later slain. After a two-hour fight, the American left gave way and the 51st, 39th, and 27th regiments were struck with dismay. The Americans retreated to their fortifications before the city. The British fleet comprising 16 vessels anchored near Fort Carroll.

While the British right was moving on land to Baltimore, their fleet comprising 50 ships entered the Patapsco river on the left to attack Fort McHenry. The fort commanded the entrance to the harbor with its narrow strait. Major George Armistead commanded the U.S. star fort defenses.

On the morning of September 12, 1814, a mass of British frigates, schooners, sloops, bomb-ketches, and bomb vessels moved to within two-and-a-half miles in front of the fort. The bomb and rocket vessels moved in closest to the fortifications on the hill. Their advance into the harbor was blocked by 24 sunken American ships lying between the fort and Lazaretto Point. These ships, scuttled to form a barrier, were later refloated at a cost of $100,000.

The American defenders in the fort and at fortifications in the harbor were comprised of one company of U.S. artillery under Captain Evans; two companies of Sea-fencibles under Captain Bunbury; two companies of volunteer "Washington Artillery" led by Captain Berry; the Baltimore Independent Artillerists led by Lieutenant Pennington; the Baltimore Fencibles; volunteer artillerists led by Judge Nicholson and; a detachment of 600 men from the 12th, 14th, 36th, and 38th U.S. regiments led by Lieutenant Colonel Stewart.

Commodore John Rodgers also led a brigade of 1,000 Marines and sailors. They were composed of survivors of Bladensburg under Captain Samuel Baron; 170 Marines stationed at Baltimore under Captain Alfred Grayson; Marines from the *Guerriere* under Captain Joseph Kuhn; Lieutenant John Harris with his Marines from Philadelphia and; the Marine artillery with 42-pounders under Captain Stiles.

At 7 a.m. the next day, 11 heavy vessels, five bomb-ships and a rocket ship opened fire on Fort McHenry. Rocket ships were a new invention and their "rockets' red glare" was used primarily as a scare tactic. A tremendous shower of shells rained down on the star fort but the Americans kept to their posts, imbued with cool courage and great fortitude. U.S. Major George Armistead gamely returned fire, but his shots fell short.

After dismantling a 24-pounder on the fort's southwest bastion by fire, the British moved three bomb vessels in closer. Now they were in range of U.S. artillery fire. In only half an hour, the British fell back after the rocket ship *Erebus* was disabled and towed back by smaller boats—but the bombardment of the fort increased until midnight. The British then moved on Fort Covinton and the City Battery manned by the Marines. The British tried to flank the fort by firing rockets and sending 1,250 Royal Marines in barges with scaling ladders to storm the fort. Two barges were sunk by Marine cannon fire and a large number of British were slain. Two hours later the British retreated. After Craney Island, this was the second time that U.S. Marines had pushed a battalion of Royal Marines back into the sea.

The shelling of Fort McHenry continued all night for 24 hours until 7 a.m. From 1,500 to 1,800 shells weighing 210 pounds each were fired. A total of 189 tons of iron burst over the fort, fragments raining down on the garrison. The concussion of the bombs was so great that houses in Baltimore were shaken to their foundations. Four Americans were killed and 24 wounded. A lucky shot fell onto the powder magazine, but fortunately it was a dud. Armistead later admitted that he alone knew that the fort's magazine was not bomb-proof. He had said nothing for he felt his men would not defend the fort if they knew.

Flag that flew over Fort McHenry

Francis Scott Key, an artillery volunteer, was seven miles away in the Bay on a truce-boat waiting for the release of an American hostage, Dr. Beanes from Upper Marlborough. Beanes had been in a cartel ship, the *Minden*, negotiating for an exchange of prisoners. After the discussion, Cochrane refused to let him or Key return until after the battle, and they were kept on the *Surprise*. That morning in the mist, Key was inspired to write the anxious National Anthem because he himself was in a state of anxiety to see "if our flag was still there!" As dawn broke, the fort's defenders defiantly replaced the weather flag with the soon-to-be "Old Glory," an enormous 30 by 42 foot American flag, snapping in the face of the departing British.

The British land army was being repulsed in front of the Baltimore fortifications. On the 12th, they lost their general, one lieutenant and 37 killed with 11 officers and 240 wounded. But since the Americans had not struck their flag, the British army planned one last effort—a night attack against Baltimore by way of the York and Harford roads.

An American officer, Colonel Brooke, had a parley with the British commander in front of the city and, amazingly, convinced him it would be futile to continue the attack against Baltimore's heavy fortifications. The British left at three a.m. on the 14th.

The Americans had lost 24 killed, 139 wounded, 50 prisoners and two guns. On the McHenry side, the Americans lost only four men killed and 24 wounded, mainly by the explosion of the shell on Nicolson's 24 pounder.

The British fleet turned around and left, to the great delight of the defenders. The fort was intact and Baltimore saved. If the city had fallen, Philadelphia and New York would surely have been burned next.

The Marines and seamen artillery under sailing-master Webster were credited by Armistead as saving both Fort McHenry and the city. The grateful citizens of Baltimore gave the Marines a gift of silver service and Commodore Rodgers proclaimed: "that the brave officers, Marines, and seamen whom I had the honor to command on that occasion did everything in their power for the defense of your city which the peculiar nature of the service and their limited means would allow is true."

Every year on September 10, Defender's Day, you can witness the re-enactment of the bombardment of Fort McHenry—a truly stirring event that recreates the feeling of that enormous British bombardment. Perhaps more than any other single battle, the defense of Fort McHenry proved the value of the Marines in assuring American victory over the British.

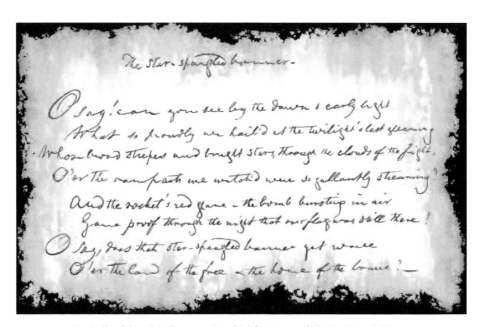

Facsimile of the original manuscript of the first stanza of *The Star Spangled Banner*

A View of the Bombardment of Fort McHenry   Print by J. Bower

Visit the Battlefield: Fort McHenry, 2400 E.Fort Ave., Baltimore, MD 21230
http.//www.nps.gov/fomc/index.htm

Chapter 16: The Battle of New Orleans

The first invasion of the continental United Sates did not occur on September 11, 2001, but on Nov. 1814. The British had planned the invasion of Louisiana for months as a decisive end to the War of 1812. They did not recognize the Louisiana Purchase, and intended the retrocession of the territory. They still had plenty of ships and troops freed up from the defeat of Napoleon, and following the burning of Washington on Nov. 26, England's forces were on the move. After their fleet picked up 9,000 troops from Jamaica, General Pakenham, Wellington's brother-in-law and a brave but inept officer, was made commanding General for the first occupying invasion on American soil.

Unlike the incursions at Lake Champlain, Baltimore and Washington, here the British planned to stay. They brought with them civil officers to run the territory with revenue collectors, clerks, printers with printing presses, and office paraphernalia. They brought empty merchant ships with the fleet to carry home booty which they estimated would be worth 14 million dollars—and they took along many officers' ladies to share in the adventure and glory. New Orleans was America's second largest port and controlled the new Louisiana territory. Occupation here would allow England to block American expansion into the west.

The U.S. campaign leading up to the battle of New Orleans actually started five months earlier on Nov. 6, 1814, with General Jackson taking Pensacola from "neutral" Spain and their British ally. Pensacola was taken with a bayonet charge by detachments of the 3rd, 39th, and 44th regiments, General Coffee's Tennesseans, Hind's battalion of Mississippi dragoons, and Choctaws—a total of 3,000 men. The Spaniards surrendered the city and left for Havana with their 400 men. The British also left, stealing 400 Spanish slaves in the process. The Americans then marched to reinforce New Orleans.

The British fleet, moving westward towards New Orleans, attacked Fort Bowyer with its command of Mobile Bay on Sept. 12, 1814, using four British ships, 90 cannon, 600 Royal Marines and 200 Indians. Even though the odds were six to one, they were repulsed by Major Lawrence and his 130 defenders with 20 cannon. The British ship *Hermes* was blown up and Major Lawrence was presented in gratitude a sword adorned with suitable emblems.

The British fleet with 60 sail then occupied Ship Island as a base for their U.S. invasion, going on to attack the American gunboat flotilla on Lake Borgne—a side approach to the city—on Dec. 14. The American flotilla was a "forlorn hope"—a term used then for a suicide mission—as they had only six small gunboats, 35 guns, 35 Marines and 182 sailors commanded by Lieutenant Thomas Ap Catesby Jones to slow the advance of the British while Jackson prepared his defenses. In a cost-saving move, President Jefferson had ordered a gunboat fleet built to go up against 1,000 British men-a-war, which were huge three-gun-deck ships. Against those odds, this gunboat fleet proved to be sheer amateur folly.

The British launched 45 barges armed with carronades and 1,200 sailors and Royal Marines setting out "to clear the lakes of the American flag." With odds of seven to one, the British were confident and rowed against a strong easterly current for 36 hours to reach the Americans at the lake.

The Americans opened fire, beginning a heated battle involving musket-to-musket, pistol-to-pistol, cutlass-to-cutlass, and man-to-man action. The battle was over in two hours and 15 minutes, with the Americans losing three Marines killed, two wounded Marines from Gunboat #156 and 35 wounded sailors. The British had lost 300 men. The "forlorn hope" had made a good showing. More important, valuable time had been bought for Jackson.

England's juggernaut kept on coming, however, landing their troops at the mouth of the Pearl River. They had no tents, the ground was drenched with dew, and the air was chilled with frost during the night, parched under the sun by day. Many on England's side—especially the West Indian troops who were not used to the cold—would die. Jackson had ordered that all the bayous leading from the ocean into the interior were to be obstructed, but a Spanish fisherman traitor showed the British a bayou to follow. They found a flank movement leading for 12 miles through Lake Pontchartrain to Villere's plantation a few miles below the city.

Captain Spencer and some of his men reconnoitered the route dressed as fishermen. From the village of Bayou Bienvenu, they paddled in a pirogue and went via Villere's Canal to the Mississippi river. They found the route easy, and the advance army of 1,600 British and two cannon followed. The army found a sharp frost that numbed the soldiers. Sir Alexander Cochrane and General Keane believed a story they heard through a captured Creole gentleman that the Americans had 12,000 men. Thus, they waited for their other brigades rather than surprise the city. The opportunity for victory was lost.

The ground went from marsh with tall reeds to more ground. Reeds gave way to wood and wood to enclosed fields. They marched through cypress, palmettos, cane brakes, vines and more. They finally reached the orange grove at the Villeres' plantation where Major Villere escaped—"catch or kill him" was the cry from the British platoon—but they couldn't catch him. He carried the news of the British Army to New Orleans.

Populated by settlers from many lands and cultures, the city was thought to hold little allegiance to the U.S. and so was considered easy pickings. The British broke through, landed at the Villeres' plantation and sent New Orleans into a panic. But the panic turned into a catalyst for resistance—everyone began running to get their rifles in working order and casting round ball.

The commander of the Royal Marines issued an order for "rape and plunder" so the citizens knew what to expect. New Orleans ladies in their coteries prepared lint and bandages. They also packed small daggers in their belts in reaction to the British war cry of "Beauty and Booty." They had heard how American women were raped in Hampton, Virginia by a contingent of foreign British troops. Jackson declared martial law in the city and every man who could hold a rifle and had four teeth to bite open a paper cartridge "volunteered" for the army. They had no choice, for Jackson vowed he would burn the city before letting it fall to the enemy. He hated the British and sported a scar on his face which he had received from a British officer's sword, when as a boy during the American Revolution, he refused to polish the officer's boots.

The inhabitants of New Orleans were an interesting mixture of people ready to resist the invader. There were French émigrés who had fought the British under Napoleon and were only too eager for another crack at the English. There were a battalion of refugees from Santo Domingo who had defended their land against the British. There were Creoles who hated the Americans but hated the British even more. And there were Baratarians who were professional smugglers adept at evading

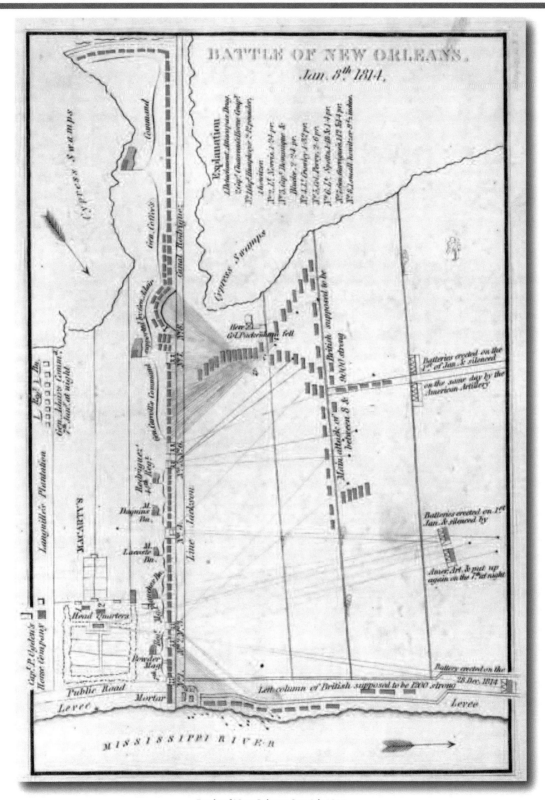

Battle of New Orleans, Jan. 8th 1814

American revenue cutters. Their captains—Dominique You and Beluche, ex-soldiers of Napoleon—would lead the pardoned pirates in manning the great guns on Line Jackson.

Many volunteer companies joined the American fight. There were Plauche's battalion—all Frenchmen, very martial, who came in running, along with a Battalion of Men of Colour under Major Daquin, and Beale's Famous Rifles, composed of young professional citizens wearing blue hunting shirts with citizen hats. All were crack shots. There were Listeau's Freemen of Color and a hundred Choctaw Indians. And when they marched they sang "Yankee Doodle" or "La Marseillaise" or "Le Chant du Depart." When the British heard them all shouting orders they thought they were fighting a huge Allied Army!

On Dec. 23, the British were two hours from the city. When Jackson heard the news he decided on a night attack. He vowed that "no British soldier would ever sleep on American soil." The schooner *Carolina* was sent at 3 a.m. to position itself against the British camp for a nighttime bombardment. Jackson led his men through the St. Charles gate accompanied by the 7th U.S. Infantry, 66 Marines under Lieutenant Francis deBellevue, Plauche's men, Gen. Coffee's 800 Tennessee mounted infantry, the Colored Battalion, U.S. artillery, Beale's men, and Hind's Troop of Mississippi dragoons with Gen. Carroll's Tennessee militia in reserve. The Tennesseans, or "Dirty Shirts' as the British condescendingly called them, wore wool hunting shirts, copper-dyed trousers, coonskin caps, and belts stuck with hunting knives and tomahawks. They were fearless and awesome militia who, armed with their Kentucky rifles, could hit a squirrel at 100 yards.

Facing them were veteran British regiments: 93rd Highland, 1,100 men; six companies of the 95th Rifles, 500; 14th Duchess of York Light Dragoons, 350; the 1st and 5th West India, 1,400 and; a rocket brigade, artillery, engineers, and sappers and miners, 1,500 for a total of 4,300 men under Major General John Keane. Added to this were General Ross' 3,000 men fresh from burning and plundering Washington; the 4th Kings Own, 750; 44th Essex, 750; 85th Buck Volunteer Light Infantry, 650; 21st Royal Fusiliers, 850—all who fought in Spain with Wellington against Napoleon.

At 7 p.m., the *Carolina* opened fire with grape and musket shot at the British camp of 1,800 men. Her captain yelled, "Give them this, for the honor of America." With deadly rapidity and precision, the terrible havoc threw the camp into blind disorder. Many British took cover under the Mississippi levee.

The Americans then attacked and the whole heavens seemed ablaze in musketry. All British discipline was lost. British officers had knots of 20 to 30 men plunging into the American ranks. General Pakenham reported, "A more extraordinary conflict has, perhaps, never occurred, absolutely hand to hand, both officers and men."

Jackson led the attack on the left. The Tennesseans, the dragoons and Beale's Rifles, skirting the edge of the swamp, hit the British on the right. Trained with the rifle since childhood, the Tennesseans fired close and didn't miss a shot. The short English musket was no match for the Yankee long bore. With no time to "fix bayonets," the British clubbed their muskets while Coffee's men used their long knives and tomahawks hand-to-hand.

The British wrestled the cannon from the artillerymen and the Marines. The Marines rallied, and with help from the 7th, retrieved their guns. With the fog rolling in, people were shooting at anything that flashed. The British had lost 247 and the Americans 213. When the 2nd British division came up, Jackson called it off.

Major Mitchell of the 95th Rifles was captured, and, much to his chagrin, his sword was surrendered to the Dirty Shirts. But the British prisoners were sent to Natchez and were lavishly treated. Jackson had the Rodriquez canal reinforced and established his HQ at the McCarty plantation. Because of the bold American action, the British thought they had fought 5,000 Yankees that night.

On the 24th, the *Louisiana* joined the *Carolina* in pounding the British camp. True to Jackson's word, the British could never get a night's rest while in front of New Orleans, and it weakened their performance.

The next day, a peace treaty was signed across the Atlantic in Ghent, Belgium, even as this bombardment raged on. Communication was slow in those days, so the men in front of New Orleans fought on unaware.

The Americans formed their line on the Rodriquez Canal—a mile long, 20 feet wide and four feet deep. It ran from the Mississippi to the swamp and a parapet was formed with cotton bales. Twelve cannon were formed into batteries and Lafitte's pirates, along with a battalion of Creole volunteers under Major Plauche, brought in much needed powder. Marine Major Daniel Carmick and 58 Marines from the New Orleans Navy Yard took position in the redoubt next to the river.

Sir Edward Pakenham arrived as the new Commander-in-Chief. Wounded many times, he was the brother-in-law of Wellington and had led the storming party at Badajoz—the toughest fight in Spain. He was knighted for his charge at Salamanca and was promised the governorship of Louisiana once taken. Wellington was offered the command of the American invasion, but refused. He wanted nothing to do with the war on America.

By the 26th, guns were brought up from the fleet to silence the two American ships. It took three days of herculean effort to slog them through the swamp and mud. The plan was to silence the ships and take the American line by storm. Cannonading on both sides commenced and in a half hour the *Carolina* blew up. The *Louisiana* was towed upriver to escape the same fate.

On the night of Dec. 27, the British in two lines moved up to within 600 yards of the American line and encamped for the night ready for a morning assault. Jackson kept reinforcing the rampart and had the levee cut to flood the river road—but the river didn't comply. Instead, the new water filled dry canals and bayous making it easier for the British to float their great guns into battery. The Americans now had 4,000 men and 20 cannon. The British had 8,000 effectives.

First Attack: The British attacked in two columns: Keane's by the levee, and General Gibbs on the right with artillery and rocket support. Rockets were a new invention primarily used as a scare tactic, especially against untried militia. But unlike Revolutionary War militia, these American sons stood their ground. The rockets only wounded two Americans and blew up two ammo caissons. "The rockets' red glare" is in our national anthem because of this timely ordnance.

The British 95th advanced on the field with the glitter of their uniforms and equipment moving as if on dress parade—a display of the majesty of power such as the Americans had never seen. The

British were blinded by their pride. They thought that their pompous display would intimidate the American militia and make them run.

The American cannons loaded with double canister—musket size balls—opened up on this wonderful spectacle. The havoc was terrible, and by noon, the first attack had failed. Marine Major Carmick was among the wounded, hit in the forehead by a rocket fragment. He died two years later from this wound. The British cannon were brought back and the army retreated to Bienvenu plantation while the Americans constructed a battery with the *Louisiana*'s guns across the river on the right bank.

Second Attack: On the night of the 31st, half of the British marched to within 400 yards of Line Jackson under newly-arrived engineer Sir John Burgoyne. Burgoyne's father had surrendered a British army at the Battle of Saratoga 38 years earlier. The British erected three demilunes with ten heavy cannon in each with ammo to last for six hours. While the Americans paraded their music, the British opened their new cannonade, setting ablaze the American rampart made from cotton bales. In return fire, the British batteries that used hogsheads of sugar as cannon emplacements were demolished. In half an hour, the American cannon had leveled the British cannon entrenchments. The English retired again for the second time.

On Jan. 1, 1815, the Marines under Lieutenant deBellevue were positioned on the right of line Jackson with the New Orleans rifles supporting Battery No. 1 and the 7th infantry, today called the Cottonbalers, on their left.

Third Attack: By now the British were drained of energy. Because of the American cannon, they had not slept for two days and nights. On Jan. 7, the British extended the Villere's canal two miles to the river by digging. The new British plan was to take the right bank, and then with enfilade fire, gain Line Jackson. They formed 10,000 men in three attack columns. Lambert, with 1,400 men, was to take the right bank; Gibbs was to storm the left of Line Jackson, and Keane the right.

Fortunately for Jackson, the 2,300-strong Kentucky militia showed up. They had traveled 1,500 miles in such a rush that only a third had rifles, and most of them were in rags. The citizens raised $16,000 to buy woolens and blankets with which the ladies would clothe them. More American reinforcements were coming in: Major General Thomas and 500 men of the 2nd Louisiana militia from Baton Rouge, and Major General Villere with 300 men of the 1st Louisiana militia from the Arcadian coast. All told, four-fifths of Jackson's men were militia.

The British had more divisions coming on line: the 7th Royal Fusiliers with 850 men; 40th Sommersetshire, 1,000; 43rd Light Infantry, 850; 44th Essex, 750; one Detachment of the 62nd, 350; Royal Marines, 1,500 and; sailors from the fleet, 2,000.

The Americans positioned 4,000 men on the left bank. Coffee's men, on the right, were extended so far into the swamp to prevent a British flank movement that they stood knee-deep in mud for days and at night slept on floating logs tied to trees. Another line was prepared a mile and a half in the rear manned by the sick and not able-bodied. A third line also was prepared by African-Americans. Four parishes loaned their negroes to work on fortifications. At the same time, the British were taking all the negroes from the plantations they occupied, for sale in the West Indies.

On Jan. 8, the attack started without a noise from the right bank. The 44th failed to bring up the ladders and fascines, made up of bundles of sticks to fill the ditch for climbing onto the American rampart. The indigent Gibbs exclaimed, "Let me live until to-morrow, and I'll hang him (Colonel Mullen of the 44th) to the highest tree in that swamp." Some historians claim the British lost the battle because of this failure.

The Americans poured on grape shot while the British fired rockets to cover the attack. The

> **Clothing the "Dirty Shirts"**
> The citizens of New Orleans contributed $16,000 for clothing the 2,300 Kentucky militia who arrived hastily in January. The ladies of the town, in one week's time, made 1,200 blanket coats or capotes, 275 waistcoats, 1,127 pairs of pantaloons, 800 shirts, 410 pairs of shoes and a great number of mattresses.

American batteries were cutting great lines through the British column from front to rear. Jackson yelled, "Stand to your guns, don't waste your ammunition, see that every shot tells," and "Give it to them boys! Let us finish this business today." The Americans had three firing lines. The first rank was the dead-shot Tennesseans, then two ranks of the newly-clad Kentuckians. Three revolving fire-lines poured out lead and iron on the redcoats. With the British now 200 yards away, the Americans were firing with deadly mechanical precision.

The British advanced on the ditch and breastwork in a case of imbecile military movement. But these were Wellington's veterans who beat Napoleon, so they advanced confidently.

At the redoubt, the Marines were at first overrun, but regained their position. Pakenham's arm was shattered and his horse killed. He then mounted a black Creole horse. Most British officers were hit and their column broke and fell back. They retreated to the swamp, reformed, took their packs off, and were again beaten back. A colonel mounting the breastwork fell dead inside the lines. The 93rd now moved forward. Stalwart Highlanders with their skirling bagpipes closed in with a 100-man front. Two Highland generals went down. Without their officers, many men faltered, but the Highlanders kept coming to a point 100 yards in front of the flaming parapet. Five hundred of the Highlanders were hit and the rest broke and fled, some crawling on all fours.

Pakenham's second horse had been downed and he was hit in the thigh by grape-shot. Hit again in the groin, he died under an oak tree that still stands on the battlefield. Gibbs and Kane were both wounded. Major Wilkinson was hit on the parapet, his body carried through the American lines where the Tennessee and Kentucky men murmured sympathy and regret to him. The British broke.

Each British regiment by now had lost two-thirds of its men. The 93rd went in 900 strong and came out with 109. The British advance in the face of murderous fire, against men they couldn't hit, was both heroic and insane. In front of the canal, 2,100 lay dead and wounded.

The battle lasted 25 minutes. The British reserve under Lambert came up, but only to cover the retreat. Surprisingly, the British had taken the right bank and captured an American flag, but the breakthrough was not exploted. By 8 a.m. the firing had stopped.

The American band played "Hail Columbia" and the Americans cheered. Then, the Americans fell silent, for as the British left the field they exposed the numerous corpses on the plain. They could not help feeling sympathy for all those unfortunate victims.

A quarter mile of British killed and disabled remained on the field. The course of the attacking columns could be traced by the red uniforms on the ground. At noon, the British asked for and were granted an armistice to bury their dead. Seven hundred were buried. Gibbs and Pakenham's bodies were encased in a barrel of spirits and shipped to England for burial. Of the 6,000 British engaged, 2,600 were lost. Amazingly, only eight Americans were killed and 63 wounded. Four hundred British wounded were taken by the Americans. By the next day, the bloody field was bare.

Over 2,000 blacks died from among the West Indian troops between January and March. Because of the wet soil; 500 Dirty Shirts died from fever and dysentery. The New Orleans hospitals being full, private homes were used for the British wounded. They were attended by quadroon (one-quarter white) nurses—the best nurses in the city.

After the armistice, the American batteries resumed fire. On Jan. 18th, Lambert asked for an exchange of prisoners. The British took nine days to leave, spiking their abandoned guns and leaving their unmovable wounded for the Americans. On the night of the 18th, the British army stealthily left the field after lighting their camp fires and erecting stuffed dummy sentinels. They marched all night and reached Lake Borgne at daybreak. General Hubert, one of Napoleon's men, said, "They are gone. There's crows sitting on the sentinels."

Lambert asked Jackson to care for the sick and wounded and if he could buy provisions for his men at New Orleans for the voyage home. Carriages were sent to comfort the enemy. On Mar. 17th, the British returned to their fleet on the lake, never to return.

When the troops reached England, they were re-embarked for Belgium to join Wellington's army for Waterloo. Gen. Lambert was knighted for gallantry at New Orleans. The state of Kentucky levied 10,000 more militia for Louisiana, in case the British returned.

Jackson had defeated the flower of Wellington's army—something Napoleon had not been able to do. The Duke of Wellington showed great admiration for Gen. Jackson and his genius after the battle, and would often inquire about him.

General Jackson commended the Marines for their valor. On Washington's Birthday, Congress passed a resolution, "Resolved That Congress entertain a high sense of the valor and good conduct of Marine Maj. Daniel Carmick, of the officers, non-commissioned officers, and Marines under his command, in the defence of the said city, on the late memorable occasion."

On Feb. 11, word reached New York that the peace had been signed in December. The entire Battle of New Orleans was fought with the war already over.

Letter from Gen. Jackson to the Rev. Abbe Dubourg:

Reverend Sir; The signal interposition of Heaven, in giving success to our arms against the enemy, who so lately landed on our shores; an enemy as powerful as inveterate in his hatred; while it must excite in every bosom attached to the happy government under which we live, emotions of the liveliest gratitude, requires at the same time some external manifestation of those feelings.

Permit me, therefore, to entreat, that you will cause the service of public thanksgiving to be performed in the cathedral, in token of the great assistance we have received from the Ruler of all events, and of our humble sense of it.

With the greatest respect,
Andrew Jackson
HQ. 7th Mil. Dist. 1/19/1815

The Battle of New Orleans   Artist: Colonel Charles H. Waterhouse, USMCR

Visit the Battlefield: Chalmette Battlefield and National Cemetery, 8606 W. St. Bernard Hwy., Chal-

Chapter 17:
Ambush at Twelve-Mile Swamp

Twelve-Mile Swamp, named for its distance from St. Augustine, Florida, is even now a forbidding area of cypress bogs and palmetto thickets. Through this heavily wooded wilderness, on the evening of Sept. 11, 1812, a ragged column of 20 Marines and Georgia militiamen passed, led by Marine Captain John Williams, a 47-year-old Virginian. His uniform was that prescribed in the 1810 regulations—navy blue coat faced with red, buttoned and laced in front with a gold epaulet on the right shoulder and counter-strap on the left; white vest and trousers with a scarlet sash; black knee-high boots; a sword at his side; and on his head, a cocked hat with cockade and plume.

Williams' mission was to escort a pair of supply wagons from the main camp of the Patriot Army near St. Augustine to the blockhouse on Davis Creek, about 22 miles to the northwest. He and his detachment had come to East Florida to join an expedition intent on annexing the Spanish province. They feared that the British would use Florida as an advance base for an invasion, and that escaped slaves might inspire insurrection in the southern states.

The Marines, half-starved, ill with fever, and their dress uniforms tattered from months of frustrating shore duty with the Army, were more than a little uneasy as they eyed the surrounding thickets. They were well aware that bands of armed Seminole Indians and runaway slaves were active in the area. Anxious to reach the safety of Davis Creek before sunset, they hurried the blue military supply wagons through the gloomy swamp as twilight deepened.

Suddenly, the woods along the trail erupted with a blaze of musket fire as a large band of Indians and blacks fired a point-blank volley into their column. Williams, his sergeant, and the lead team of horses were downed by the first shots. The wounded captain was quickly assisted off the trail by one of his men.

Distinguished in their blue coats, white trousers, and high-crowned shakos, Williams' Marines took up defensive positions along the trail and returned fire with their standard-issue 1808 smoothbore, muzzle-loading, flintlock muskets. The badly wounded Capt. Williams watched as Captain Tomlinson Fort, his militia counterpart from Milledgeville, Georgia, took over the command, exhorting the troops to continue the fight until the last cartridge. Eventually, he too was wounded, and ordered a retreat further into the swamp. As the fighting ended, the enemy band destroyed one wagon and drove off in the other, with their wounded inside.

During the night, part of the detachment made its way to the blockhouse while Williams, too severely wounded to be moved, hid himself among the palmetto thickets. The next morning, a rescue force found the Marine captain—his left arm and right leg broken, and his right arm, left leg and abdomen pierced by musket fire. Searching further, they found six more wounded in the brush, in addition to Williams' sergeant, stripped and scalped.

"You may expect," Williams wrote to Lieutenant Colonel Marine Commandant Franklin Wharton four days later, "that I am in a dreadful situation, tho' I yet hope I shall recover in a few months." Despite being moved to the relative comfort of a nearby plantation house, Williams died on Sept. 29.

The ambush at Twelve-Mile Swamp and the subsequent death of Marine Capt. John Williams proved to be the catalyst which brought an end to an ill-conceived and diplomatically embarrassing American scheme to annex Spanish East Florida by force.

Seminole Chief Osceola (1804–1838)

Swamp Ambush   Artist: Colonel Charles H. Waterhouse, USMCR

Visit the Battlefield: 12 Mile Swamp Recreation Area, Florida International Golf Parkway, West of

Chapter 18: Attack of Fajardo Bay

Although the United States would not declare war with Spain until 74 years later, at this time Spanish pirates operated unchecked in the Caribbean. Their safe haven was the Spanish Main: an area that today ranges from Nicaragua to Panama. U.S. naval vessels patrolled these waters to deter pirates from attacking American commerce. At 8 a.m. on Jan. 14, 1824, the American schooners *Grampas* and *Beagle* entered Fajardo Bay, on the east end of Puerto Rico, a Spanish possession and a pirate stronghold.

On board were 200 sailors and Marines under Captain David Porter, who tried to exact an apology for an insult given Navy Lieutenant Charles Platt and the American flag a month before. The two ships anchored opposite a steep 80-foot cliff overlooking the bay. Atop, the Spanish had erected a gabion fort—earth held by woven sticks—and had two 18-pounder bronze cannons. The ten-man battery was seen loading and aiming their guns on the *Grampas*. Capt. Porter ordered Marine Lieutenant Thomas Barton and his 14-man Marine guard to attack the two-gun battery, take the fort, spike the guns, and destroy the ammunition. Marines were extensively trained as replacement cannon crews for the great guns—24 and 30 pound cannons. On board U.S. frigates, if a navy cannon crew was taken out, a Marine squad would jump in and work the guns.

Barton's Marines climbed the steep cliff and flanked the battery. Without his cover—called a *shako*—and armed with two pistols, Barton peered over the crest of the cliff where a fuse was lit alongside one unmanned gun. The attacking Marines were dressed in white linen overalls, single-breasted blue coats with red and yellow lace, black beaver shakos with a red plush plume, and carried 1817 Hall muskets with bayonets, pistols and cutlasses.

Over the top, Barton and his Marines took the abandoned two-gun battery. One cannon was loaded with round shot, canister consisting of grape shot, musket balls, and nails. The other cannon was partly charged. The guns were spiked by inserting a tapered file into the touch-hole and breaking off the tip. The ammunition was destroyed. After securing the battery, Barton's men re-embarked and joined the main body of Marines and sailors who landed near the road leading to Fajardo town.

The main body of 200 men led by Lieutenant Haratio Crabbe's 24 Marines and two drummers marched under a flag of truce towards the town. Near the town, they met the *alcalde*—the municipal judge and captain of the port, who offered Lt. Platt an apology and offered the men refreshments. Afraid that the Marines' drinking would get out of control, Porter refused the offer and ordered his men to return. Back in the U.S., Porter was charged at a court martial at the Marine barracks in Washington. He was charged with committing hostile acts against Spanish subjects and disobedience of orders. Before him was arrayed the cream of the Navy.

Marine Lieutenant Thomas Barton took the stand to testify on the events at Fajardo. Porter was sentenced to six months' suspension of his commission, and was praised at the same time by the court for his zeal in dealing with the pirates.

Foray into Fajardo Bay   Artist: Colonel Charles H. Waterhouse, USMCR

Visit the battlefield: puertoricodaytrips.com/laguna-grande-fajardo-biobay/

Chapter 19:
Fighting Pirates at Quallah Battoo

Less than ten degrees north of the equator, on the island of Sumatra, lies the rich pepper-growing region of Acheh. Beginning in the 1790s, New England trading ships would stop along the island's western coast to exchange Spanish silver for the spice, needed not only to flavor and preserve food, but for the lucrative trans-Atlantic trade with Europe.

American ships, based primarily in Salem, had made nearly a thousand voyages carrying away 370 million pounds of pepper worth 17 million dollars at wholesale—almost half the pepper produced in Acheh during this period. A pound of pepper then sold for $13.

The American ships were faster, and the Dutch and British disliked their competition in this lucrative business. They pressured the Sultan of Acheh, Muhammed Shaw, to detain American ships in violation of trading laws. The British went so far as to try to entirely exclude American trade from Acheh. It is unclear how much of the piracy on American ships was pure robbery and how much was influenced by the colonial power games of the period.

In January 1831, one of these American merchant vessels—the *Friendship*—dropped anchor off the Sumatran town of Quallah Battoo to take on a load of pepper. A band of Malay pirates in three proas, or ships, boarded the *Friendship*, murdered a large part of the crew, looted the cargo and drove the craft ashore. Their plunder included four chests of opium which was used in medicine, and 18,000 Spanish dollars.

The Malay pirate fleets along the Straits of Malaka were considered the "Vikings of the East." Their proas were 50 feet long, fast, and nimble, using both oars and light sails, and were armed with swivel guns mounted on bulkheads. The pirates, dressed in scarlet and chain-mail, brandished krises—a sword with a wavy blade—two-handed swords, and flintlocks. They were famous for either murdering every soul on board, or selling the few survivors to slavery.

The Captain of the *Friendship*, Charles Endicott, had been ashore during the attack. When he made a complaint to the local chieftain, Mahomet, insult was added to injury for Mahomet then put a price on the head of both the Captain and his officers. With the help of a friendly native chief, Po Adam, Endicott enlisted the help of three other merchant captains who agreed to help him recover his vessel. Although the ship was recaptured and returned, her owners sent a vigorous protest to President Andrew Jackson demanding retribution.

President Jackson declared that "a daring outrage" had been committed on the seas of the East Indies involving the "plunder" of one of its merchantmen engaged in the pepper trade at a port in Sumatra. There appeared to be no room for diplomatic action, as Jackson believed that "the piratical perpetrators belonged to tribes in such a state of society that the usual course of proceedings between civilized nations cannot be pursued. I forthwith dispatched a frigate with orders to require immediate satisfaction for the injury and indemnity to the sufferers."

At New York, the frigate *Potomac*, equipped with forty-two 32-pounder cannon, was rigged and ready to sail for the punitive expedition. The frigate had orders to "inflict chastisement" and carried a detachment of Marines and three detachments of seamen under Commodore Downes to punish the natives for their treachery.

Originally under orders to proceed to China via Cape Horn and the Pacific, the *Potomac*'s route was changed to the Cape of Good Hope and the Indian Ocean as a result of the protest by the *Friendship*'s owners and the outcry from the general public. On Feb. 5, after sailing for five months, the *Potomac*, disguised as a Danish East Indiaman, anchored five miles off Quallah Battoo.

At 2 a.m. the next day, 282 Marines and sailors embarked on the ship's boats and hit the beach for the attack. Divided into groups, the men were assigned to each of the four forts guarding the town. At dawn, the column led by Marine Lieutenants Alvin Edson and George Terrett moved forward. The Marines heading for Tuko de Lima nestled in the jungle behind the town.

Within minutes of the Marine approach, the Malays were alerted and the fighting became intense. The enemy met the Marines with cannon, muskets and blunderbusses (early shotguns). Charging forward, the Marines' "superior discipline and ardor seemed fully to compensate for their want of numbers." They broke through the outer walls, blew up the stockade gate, and captured the fort. Edson, with a small guard, pushed through the town to join in the attack on the remaining fort.

As smoke from the other forts drifted overhead, Edson, his Marines, and a detachment of sailors smashed through the bamboo walls of Duramond's fort and engaged the kris-wielding Malays. Dressed in full blue uniform, Lt. Edson parried the lunge of a defender with his Mameluke sword while a Marine at his side parried with his bayonet. In this hand-to-hand combat with the Marines, the Malays fought to the death. Within minutes, the fort was taken, with only a few Malays left to flee into the jungle.

With the forts dismantled, the town ablaze, a few Malays hiding in the jungle, and the surf rising, the Marines and sailors were recalled. Over 150 Malay pirates, including Mahomet, were killed, with the Americans suffering just one sailor and two Marines killed and 11 wounded.

This successful attack would deter the Malays and others from similar aggressions for quite some time. In addition to their skill with cold steel, the Americans had emerged victorious due to their long-range, light-caliber cannon and their ability to deliver rapid rifle fire.

Under cover of a Marine guard, the boats embarked for the *Potomac*. Later in the day, all hands gathered on deck to witness the burial of their three shipmates killed in the attack.

Other rajas from nearby states sent delegations to the ship pleading that Downes spare them from the same fate they had suffered at Quallah Battoo. Downes informed them that if any American ships were attacked again, the same treatment would be given to the perpetrators.

The next morning, the *Potomac* moved within a mile of Quallah Battoo, ran out her long 32-pounder cannon and bombarded the town, killing another 300 natives before raising sail and heading for sea. This was the first-ever official U.S. military intervention in Asia. This was the second time—after Tripoli—that the Marines had been called in to protect American business and retaliate for the murder of American citizens.

It is interesting to note that 180 years later, American forces are once again engaged in similar situations with modern-day pirates off the coast of Somalia.

Marines attack the town

Quallah Battoo   Artist: Colonel Charles H. Waterhouse, USMC

Visit the Battlefield: Quallah Battoo is located 150 miles SE from the tip of the Acheen peninsula, Sumatra.

Chapter 20:
Marines in the 2nd Seminole War

In the summer of 1835, Commandant Colonel Henderson marched his Marine battalion south to join the Creek war. Legend has it that he had left the Marine barracks in Washington with a note tacked on his HQ door, "Gone to fight the Indians. Will be back when the war is over." In fact, they arrived too late for the fight and spent the rest of the summer patrolling the Georgia/Alabama border on foot and by steamboat.

They joined Lieutenant Colonel Freeman's battalion, and on Oct. 28, took command at Fort Brooke near Tampa, Florida. The two battalions were reorganized into one regiment of six companies comprising more than half the strength of the entire Corps. They were joined by 750 Creek Indian volunteers with Marine officers commanding some of the Creek units. This was the Corps' first experience leading native troops.

Commanding General Alexander Macomb had only four major generals at the outbreak of the Second Seminole War. Major Generals Edmund Gaines and Winfield Scott had failed in their mission due to insufficient planning and difficult terrain and climate. Major General Thomas Jesup was the last of the senior officers to attempt defeating the Seminoles.

The word *Seminole* is from the Creek word *simanooli*, meaning runaway. These runaway Creeks were survivors from the battle of Horseshoe Bend in 1812, and they refused to join the Creek migration to the new Indian Territory later called Oklahoma. They escaped south to Florida to get away from the whites, thinking that the swampland would be impassable for pursuit. The British continued to encourage Seminole raiding parties long after official cessation of the War of 1812, in 1814.

Jesup had just suppressed a Creek uprising in western Georgia and eastern Alabama—the campaign known as the Creek War of 1836—and decided to try a new approach to the fight in Florida. Rather than using large columns to force the Seminoles into fighting a large, set battle, he concentrated on "search and destroy" tactics—wearing the Indians down with small attacks that threatened their families and sources of supply. The Indians' tactics were "hit and run" and they melted away in seconds into the swamp refuge if the enemy was too formidable.

The Seminoles lived in "hammocks" which was a patch of ground rising above the swamp and waterways, covered with saw-grass. Having a network of hammocks provided the Indians hundreds of acres for growing foodstuffs and pasture land. Finding the enemy in this lair of swampland was a major challenge. These same frustrating tactics were employed by the Viet Cong 130 years later.

The Army made repeated sorties into the Great Waboo Swamp without success. The Allied Creeks, wearing white turbans to distinguish them from the enemy in battle, led the pursuit. In one attack, Marine Lieutenant Andrew Ross, who held the rank of Captain in the Creek unit, was shot while trying to cross a stream. He died of his wounds on December 11, 1836, the first Marine officer to be killed in action since the end of the War of 1812.

When Brig. Gen. Jesup took over the war, he mustered a force of over 9,000 men, half of which were Army regulars, plus a battalion of Marines consisting of 38 officers and 400 enlisted Marines. He reorganized the Army of the South into two brigades and on Jan. 8, 1837, gave Marine Col. Henderson command of the 2nd Brigade which included the Marines. Lieutenant Colonel Samuel Miller was given responsibility to guard the convoys moving between Tampa Bay and the Army depots on the military road to Fort King.

On Jan. 23, near Lake Abapopka, a detachment including Captain John Harris' company of "Horse Marines" fought a large body of Seminoles. Five days later, Col. Henderson led a force into the Great Cypress Swamp to find the main body of Indians.

When the Allied Creeks made contact with the Seminoles, Henderson ordered the Marines into the battle. In the dense swamp, the Marines and the Creeks engaged the enemy across the Hatchee-Lustee River, a deep 20-yard-wide stream. Marines and soldiers extended along the river bank to lay a crossfire. When the enemy's fire slackened, the troops plunged over, swimming or crossing on logs. Capt. Harris was one of the first across. The enemy fell back. Mounted Marines captured some women and children along with 100 pack ponies and 1,400 head of cattle—but the warriors escaped into the swamp taking their wounded with them. Marine Private Joel Wright was killed in the crossing and three others were wounded.

Henderson's force pursued the enemy for half a mile through an even more difficult stretch. The Seminoles made repeated stands, but Henderson could never catch up with the enemy's main body. Even so, the Battle of the Hatchee-Lustee was the Marine's largest battle of the war. Six Marines had been KIA—including Marine Drummer Thomas Peterson—or died later of wounds.

Having lost their families and their main source of food, the Seminoles agreed to a parley in March with the chiefs consenting to a truce and removal to the west. On March 6, an armistice was signed. Many chiefs, including Micanopy, had surrendered but the two important leaders—Osceola and the aged Arpiucki (also known as Sam Jones)—had not come in and were very opposed to relocation. The Indians agreed to assemble at Fort Brooke for removal; it looked as though the war was over.

Henderson was promoted to brevet Brigadier General, the first Marine to hold a general officer rank. Captains William Dulany and Harris were made brevet majors. Henderson returned to Washington in May and Brevet Lt. Col. Miller was left in command of the troops south of the Hillsborough River. His force included 189 Marines at Tampa Bay, where the Seminoles began to concentrate for removal. Everyone was convinced the war was finished.

Then, at midnight on June 2, Osceola recaptured the compliant chiefs and their 700 followers at the poorly guarded fort, and forced them to leave the Marine encampment before dawn. The war began again and continued for five more years.

In October, a parley was formed with Osceola, the chief fire-brand, and Coeehajo, who were both seized after being tricked by a false flag of truce. Osceola died of malaria three months later at Fort Moultrie, Charleston, at the age of 33. Another battle was fought at Lake Okeechobee on Christmas Day.

In the summer of 1838, a special naval force was organized from small ships and dugout canoes. The unit won the nickname "Mosquito Fleet." By 1841, it had 652 men including 130 Marines.

The war dragged on intermittently, employing unusual tactics. In 1839, Brigadier General Walter Armistead, in one of his "search and destroy" missions, obliterated over 500 acres of Seminole crops. Col. Harvey, in another attack, had his men dress as Seminoles to bait a trap. He received $55,000 from Congress to bribe Seminole chiefs to bring in their bands. Braves were given $500 to come in and move west, females were paid $100. American victory was eventually achieved by a combination of the destruction of Seminole food resources and plain bribery.

The Navy began to take a larger role in the war. In late 1839, command of the Mosquito Fleet on the east coast passed from Lieutenant Powell to Lieutenant McLaughlin, USN. Based at Tea Table Key in the upper Florida Keys, this force was intended to interdict Cuban and Bahamian traders bringing arms and munitions to the Seminoles. Schooners patrolled offshore and barges ranged closer to the mainland.

In addition, smaller boats and 140 dugout canoes manned by sailors and Marines probed the Everglades and up-river. In December of 1840, Marines in dugouts crossed the Everglades from east to west and were the first white men to make this journey.

In 1841, with Col. Worth now in command, the conduct of this war was costing the US $1,116,000 a year. Worth finally received permission from Congress to allow the remaining Seminoles to be left in peace if they stayed in the southwest part of southern Florida. Seminole bands remaining in Florida included some led by Holata Mico (nicknamed "Billy Bowlegs"); Arpicochi; Chipco; and the black Seminole leader Thlochlo Tustenuggee or "Tiger-Tail." The mixed-blood black chiefs were especially determined to continue the fight—to them, death was better than a return to hard, coastal slavery. This was the first time blacks had fought in a war for their freedom.

Although the Seminole Wars went on for more than 40 years, the last Seminoles living in the Everglades never surrendered to the U.S. forces: a lasting testament to Indian bravery and determination. A total of 1,466 men and 61 Marines were killed or died of malaria in the Florida war.

The 2nd Seminole War was the first of many Expeditionary Force operations for which the U.S. Marines would become justly famous.

U.S. Marines searching for the Indians among the mangroves during the Seminole War

Visit the Battlefield: http://www.floridastateparks.org/fortfoster/default.cfm

Chapter 21:
Marine Conductors on the Trail of Tears

In 1830, the Federal government ordered some 60,000 southwest Indians from what was then Mississippi, Alabama and Georgia to relinquish their ancestral land and move west to the new Indian Territory, now Oklahoma. They were the five so-called "civilized tribes"—Choctaws, Chickasaws, Creeks, Cherokees and Seminoles.

This order was done under the Indian Removal Act, passed by President Andrew Jackson, because some 10,000 white settlers and greedy land speculators coveted the Indian land. The underlying reason was "King Cotton" which thrived in this southern climate and became an enormous cash crop.

These Indians were a very advanced people. They grew cotton, carded it and made their own cloth, much to the chagrin of the uncouth settlers. The Indian Removal Act was thought to be the most expedient solution to expel the tribes from this valuable land.

Having to move thousands of Indians some 1,225 miles west in the winter was a tall order for the Marines. A forced movement of so many under adverse conditions had never before been attempted. The suffering of the Indians has been described as horrific, but the Marines conducting them devoted themselves indefatigably to aid and comfort the wretched marchers. The Choctaws of southeastern Mississippi were the first to be removed, followed by some of the Seminoles.

The Choctaw chief Pushmataka couldn't believe what was happening to his peaceful people. Parting with the land they had lived on for centuries, "where we have grown up as the herbs of the woods," was incomprehensible to the Indians.

The Chickasaws moved west themselves with no apparent problems. They and the Choctaws would experience good conditions compared to the tribes that followed.

As it turned out, the Indian removal would become one of the darkest chapters in American conscience and history: truly, an American tragedy.

The government justified its actions by events that had taken place over the preceding years. In the summer of 1813, the Creeks, encouraged by Tecumseh and supplied by the British and the Spaniards in Florida, massacred the Fort Mims garrison in southeast Alabama killing all 400 men, women and children. The black slaves taken were now Creek slaves. Many of the Creeks then went to Pensacola with their American scalps and redeemed their reward from the British agents there.

General Andy Jackson destroyed the Creek will to fight in the Battle of Horseshoe Bend in 1814—out of 1,000 Creek warriors only 70 escaped. After this defeat, the Creeks didn't want to fight the whites any more. They realized that they were as many "as the leaves in the forest." The men became idle and superstitious while their slaves did all the work. One band of Creeks, the Yuchi, rose up in Alabama but the Marines, some armed with the new Colt rifles, put down that insurrection.

The survivors of Horseshoe Bend joined the Seminoles in Florida where the Indian leader Osceola roused his warriors to resist. The son of an English trader and a Creek mother, Osceola would become the Marines' greatest opponent. Osceola repeatedly attacked U.S. Army units with brilliant tactics. The whole peninsula was shaken in fear. Runaway Negro slaves who had escaped from Southern plantations joined the Seminoles in the fight. The scattered U.S. Army numbering only 4,000 soldiers needed help. Colonel Henderson volunteered the Marine Corps and President Jackson—who had earlier tried to abolish the Corps—accepted readily.

The first Marines to join the Seminole War were 57 men under First Lieutenant Nathanuel Waldron of the frigate *Constitution*. They landed on Jan. 22, 1836 at Fort Brooke near Tampa. (For more on the Seminole Wars, see Chapter 20.)

In the spring of 1836, Commandant Archibald Henderson led the Marines to fight the Indians who had started an uprising against the planned march west of the Mississippi.

On June 23rd, Henderson reported with 462 Marines to Major General Winfield Scott at Columbus, Georgia. They had marched 224 miles across the state in 14 days. The next day, 160 more Marines from New York under Lieutenant Colonel William Freeman reached Milledgeville and headed south to Florida.

The Marines conducted company-sized patrols, guarded the mail road from Columbus to Tuskegee, Alabama, and supervised one of the many concentration camps built. The Creeks were gathered in from two areas of Alabama. The upper towns in Northeast Alabama numbered 14,142 Indians with 445 slaves. The lower towns in Southeast Alabama had 8,552 Creeks with 457 slaves. Though most of their cattle and horses had been stolen by the whites, the Indians' slaves were surprisingly permitted to accompany them to the new land.

 The Creeks sold 5.2 million acres in Alabama at roughly one-sixth of market value. Some of the Creeks not obeying the removal crossed over into Georgia and moved in with the Cherokees. They never recuperated from their losses and lived in abject poverty.

The Indians received their worst treatment in the state of Alabama where the white intruders rampantly engaged in every form of oppression. The state government sided with the land speculators and in the investigation of fraud uncovered by the Federals, the state enforced its law preventing an Indian from testifying against a white. Though the U.S. Supreme Court had ruled in favor of the Indians, Jackson ignored the court's decision.

The Creek uprising in 1836 actually was propagated by the whites to mask the Federal investigation of fraudulent land claims. The Georgia militia had fired on the Creeks and the most belligerent band, the Yuchi, retaliated—so the burning and killing started anew.

Creek husbands, brothers and fathers were asked to serve in Florida against the Seminoles, much as the Japanese-American 443rd Regimental Combat Team served against Germany in WWII, while back at home, their property was destroyed, girls were raped and some Creeks were abducted as slaves by the whites.

Even though General Scott had ordered, "Every possible kindness…must be shown by the troops," the troops, except for the Marines, didn't obey and the roundup proved harrowing. Families were separated. The elderly and ill were forced out at gunpoint. People were given only moments to collect cherished possessions. White looters then followed, ransacking homesteads as the Creeks were led away.

In Tallahassee, the southern Creeks were collected for removal. In July, 15,000 Creeks started the "Trail of Tears" to today's Oklahoma. On Sept. 5, 1836, Marine Lieutenant John Sprague led the detachment of 1984 Creeks under Chief Tusk-e-batch-e-hadjo across Alabama to Memphis. Tusk-e-batch-e-hadjo was appalled at what the interlopers were doing to his people.

The whites appropriated everything: fields and crops, horses, saddles, harnesses, hoes, rifle guns, chickens, hogs, cows and calves, ducks, geese, money, grist mills, feather beds, blankets, quilts, pots, ovens, kettles, dishes, cups and saucers, knives and forks, pails, gardens, bacon, potatoes, beans, salt, cabins, looms, shuttles, weaver's reeds, spinning wheels, thread reels, bedsteads, tables, chairs, cupboards, spoons, plows, chairs, baskets, saws, shovels, carpenter's tools—even fiddles. Every necessity to maintain human life was stolen by the looters. Not even bedding was left for the Indian children. It was a cruel way to start a 1,000-mile trip.

The removal was under the auspices of the Alabama Emigrating Company whose contractors were to meet the trek at intervals with supplies. They were always late and people starved as a result. The contractors saw this as a chance to profit at the expense of these hapless Creeks. The Army, trying to help, brought in pork and flour that had spoiled from basking in the hot sun for days. Oftentimes, the Indians had to go into the forest to eat dead animals.

In Lt. Sprague's wagon train were 1,984 Indians, 45 wagons for the children and the sick, and 500 warriors on horses. One hundred and fifty hostiles from the Creek war came in from a swamp. They kept to the back of the column and, fearing retaliation, stayed quiet. No fodder was provided for the horses and many died in route. The cane brake that flourished along rivers was the only feed that sustained the herd—when they were lucky enough to chance upon on it.

They averaged 12 miles a day. Sprague sent 500 men on their ponies through the huge Mississippi Swamp and arranged for the bulk of his party to go by boat up the Arkansas River to Little Rock. Eventually, 13,000 Creeks assembled near Memphis to cross the Mississippi River. The Indians were afraid of going on the steamboats for fear of being thrown overboard if they died, as burial rites were very sacred to them. As it turned out on a later trek, 311 Creeks drowned when the steamboat *Monmouth* broke in half after a collision with another boat.

Across the Mississippi, game was now abundant as the land was clear of habitation. On Nov. 22, the group arrived at Fort Gibson, Oklahoma. They had marched 800 miles by land, and traveled 425 miles by water in 96 days. Twenty-nine Indians died on the trail, many of them without a garment to cover their nakedness.

On subsequent marches, conducted by the Army, the suffering endured by the Creeks on the trail was immensely worse. The change of climate, absence of doctors, lack of nutrition, exhaustion and brutal treatment would add up to a death each day on the long march. First to succumb were children, the weak, the aged, the infirm and the intemperate. When passing near a white settlement, they were besieged by settlers who sold them whiskey. The Indians had a propensity for liquor and their binges slowed up the march for days as they tried to drown their misery.

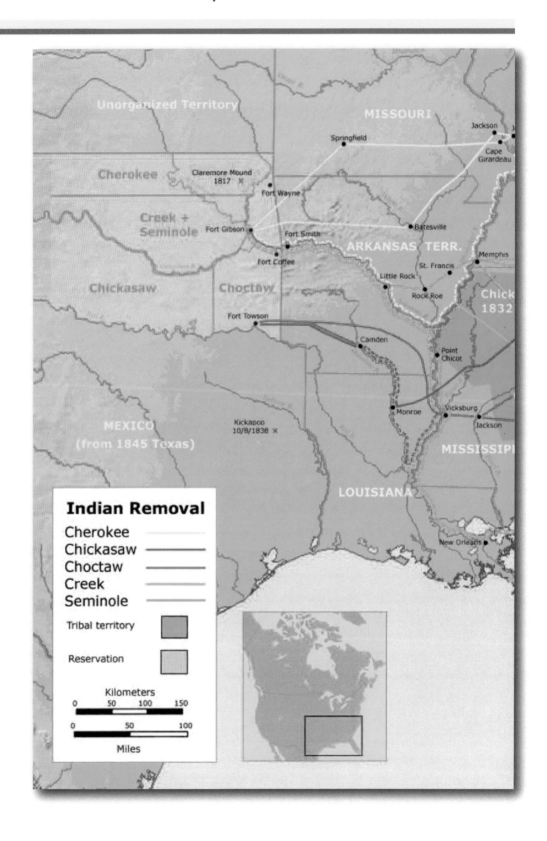

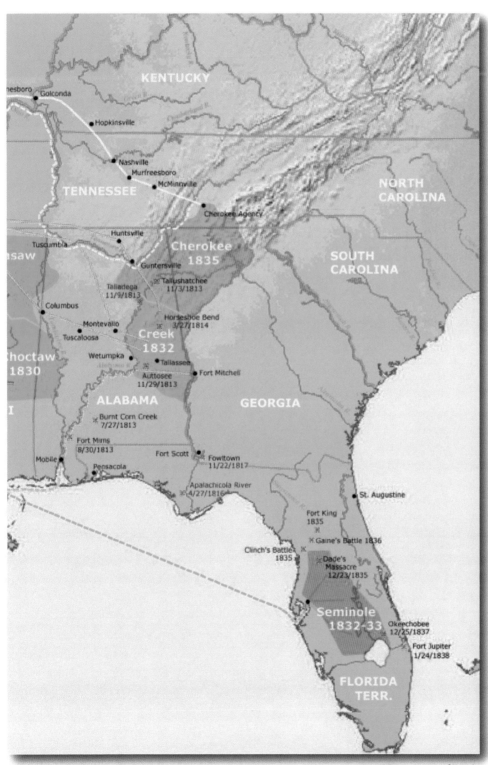

Map courtesy of Demis

Departing in the summer, the Indians wore only a single cotton garment and froze when winter came with only one blanket issued to each family. Some of them marched in chains. Two days' rations were issued every other day, with corn issued every day. The Creek women cut holes in fallen trees where they pounded their maize. Since their land was forcibly sold far below its value, and no crops had been allowed to be harvested, they had no means to buy the necessary supplies for the trek. Marching barefoot through cold, sleeting storms they marched on frozen ground which also took its toll on their all-wooden carts. No iron or forges were available to repair them.

Their trail was obviously marked by the thousands of vultures who followed their route. Indians who died were laid by the side of the road, covered with branches, their worn-out bodies to be eaten by wolves that scattered their bones everywhere. An estimated 3,400 Creeks died in the combined marches to Oklahoma.

The Indians under Sprague's care had been fortunate to have the sympathetic Marine lieutenant in charge. His Marines tried to make the Indians' journey as comfortable as possible, doing everything they could short of paying for necessities out of their own pockets. They wrote to him, thanking him for his kindness.

> "You have been with us many moons….You have heard the cries of our women and children…our road has been a long one….Tell General Jackson if the whites will let us, we will live in peace and friendship….We are men….we have women and children, and why should we come like wild horses?"

A piteous outcry from a tragic people. If this was payback for the Fort Mims massacre, the Creeks paid for it many times over. It was one of the most difficult duties the Marines were ever made to conduct.

Visit the Trail of Tears: www. nps.gov/trte/index.html
Fort Gibson, OK (terminus of Marine column) 918.478-4088

Chapter 22:
Marine Special Ops Take California

Mexico had achieved independence from Spain in 1821, but during the 12 years prior to 1846, four revolutions took place in the province of California. By the eve of the war with the U.S., California had become an independent republic.

New Mexico, like priceless California, was so far removed from the Mexican capitol that for years Mexican control was very ineffective. Its people had little commerce with Mexico and for a long time St. Louis was their main trading partner. Both provinces were ripe for plucking and President Polk was ready to annex these two plums.

Before the Mexican War began, President Polk already had his eye on conquering California (before he contemplated buying it for 25 million dollars). Texas had accepted admittance as a state of the Union on July 4, 1845, and Polk wanted to expand its boundaries. He especially wanted California for the U.S. if war should break out with Mexico.

On the night of October 30, 1845, Polk held a secret meeting in the White House with Marine First Lieutenant Archibald Gillespie, who Navy Secretary Bancroft regarded as an accomplished and most trustworthy officer. Gillespie had been chosen to deliver the orders for invasion. He carried secret, memorized instructions to Thomas Larkin, the U.S. consul at Monterey, dispatches for Commodore John Sloat on the west coast, and personal letters to Army Lieutenant John Fremont who was "exploring" the far west for the Army's Topographical Corps.

Sloat's orders were "once war was declared to occupy ports as your force may permit." All three men were ordered to use guile, infiltration and subversion to acquire California for the U.S. when the opportunity presented itself. As it turned out, each of the three carried out their orders in various ways.

Pio Pico, the California governor from Los Angeles, was often at odds with Jose Castro, the self-appointed military chief in Monterey. The province was governed so poorly that the Californios actually wanted to be acquired, preferably by the U.S. instead of England or Russia. The Californios considered the U.S. "the happiest and freest nation in the world destined soon to be the most wealthy and powerful." The Americans in turn were impressed with the scale of the Californios' industry. Some hacienda livestock totaled 2,000 horses, 15,000 cattle, and 20,000 sheep; albeit, this wealth had been obtained by the slave labor of 11 million Indians. Nonetheless, Pico settled his differences with Castro and set about forming an army to resist the American freebooters.

Traveling in disguise, Gillespie went via Vera Cruz, Mexico City and Mazatlan—where he located Commodore Sloat—and reached Monterey in April, 1846. He delivered his messages to Larkin and then went north until he met Fremont at Klamath Lake in May. Two days later, Polk urged Congress to recognize that "war exists." It did so, and newly breveted Army Brigadier General Stephen Kearny, an 1812 veteran at Fort Leavenworth, was ordered to "conquer and take possession of California."

Fremont and Gillespie rode south into California with rugged American settlers wearing buckskin and carrying rifles and long bowie knives. Gillespie, guarded by 12 Delaware Indians, went ahead to San Francisco Bay and there obtained powder, 8,000 percussion caps, and lead for 9,000 bullets from

Commander Montgomery. Numbering 700, this group made up the largest foreign contingent in California.

In June, under attack at Sonoma, American settlers proclaimed the California "Bear Flag" Republic. Fremont took charge of the military force of the "one-village" nation and Gillespie became his executive officer in charge of training the "Bear Flag Army" into effective fighters. The Bear Flag was designed by William Todd, whose aunt had recently married a country lawyer named Abraham Lincoln. Fremont, without authority, had started a revolution without knowing war had been declared with Mexico. He then took his forces south to Monterey to start the rebellion there.

Commodore Sloat ordered the sloop-of-war *Portsmouth*, under Commander Montgomery, to Monterey to protect American lives and property. On July 7, he officially invaded California for the U.S., sending Captain William Mervine, U.S.N., ashore at Monterey with 85 marines and 165 sailors commanded by Marine Captain Ward Marston. They raised the American flag over the customs house and Second Lieutenant William Maddox stayed ashore with a Marine detachment as a garrison—the west coast's first Marine Corps post. Northern California was now in American hands.

Two days later, the Bear Flag Republic became American and Montgomery, along with Second Lieutenant Henry Watson, landed with 14 Marines to occupy Yerba Buena (San Francisco). San Francisco was already loaded with Americans as the U.S. whaling fleet in the Pacific numbered 650 vessels with 17,000 commercial sailors rotating through their San Francisco base.

Back in New Mexico, Kearny's force from Fort Leavenworth was on the march, and it was said that "the world is coming with him." He had 1,458 men, 459 horses, 3,658 draft mules, and 14,904 cattle and oxen. His artillery consisted of twelve 6-pounders and four 12-pound howitzers. He was able to take Santa Fe bloodlessly after the officers of the New Mexican army of 4,000 Mexicans and Indians under Manuel Pico decided to give up without a fight. The senoritas were frightened of the rough-looking American occupiers but Kearny threw a big "kick-up" dance until dawn, and the local ladies recovered their composure. Kearny then set out for California with 300 dragoons, who were heavy cavalry. On the march, they encountered Kit Carson, "the celebrated mountain man," who was on his way to Washington with an express from Stockton and Fremont announcing that they had taken California. Kearny sent 200 of his dragoons back to New Mexico and persuaded Kit Carson to return with him to California as a guide. They marched on to take control of the Pacific province.

The Californios, nearly all Mexican, didn't really care who was running the territory as long as their dignity and sensibilities prevailed. However, the superior attitude exhibited by the conquering Americans caused many problems.

When Commodore Stockton took over command from Sloat, he legitimized Fremont and Gillespie and their 160 mounted men as the "California Battalion of Mounted Riflemen." Stockton issued a proclamation annexing California to the U.S. In retaliation, Castro's force moved on Los Angeles to join forces with Pico.

Stockton wanted to invade western Mexico, so he ordered Fremont to expand the California Battalion to 300 men to replace the sailors garrisoned along the coast.

The plan now was for Fremont to land in San Diego and march north in a pincer movement, while Stockton would land at San Pedro, 35 miles below Los Angeles, and march south to crush the Californios led by Pico and Castro. Stockton sent the battalion south by ship to San Diego to cut off the Mexicans operating near Los Angeles. It, plus some 80 Marines, raised the American flag at San Diego on July 30. Stockton sent a party including First Lieutenant Jacob Zeilin and his Marine detachment ashore to hold Santa Barbara. The Commodore then seized San Pedro, the port of Los Angeles, with a force of sailors and Marines. He proclaimed the California port part of the U.S. and established a curfew on the residents.

Stockton entered Los Angeles on August 12 with 360 Marines and sailors, and Fremont arrived with a 120 horsemen. Gillespie stayed to hold San Diego with 48 Marines. Before Stockton sailed to Acapulco to join the Army, he named Fremont the Military Governor of California, and Gillespie as Commandant Captain of the Southern District, the center of Mexican influence.

Commandant Gillespie moved to Los Angeles and, without any experience, ruled with an iron hand. He held the Californios in contempt and treated them rudely. He initiated a form of martial law where he outlawed reunions in houses and forbade even two people to walk in the street together. Worse, the Americans were undisciplined and as a result the Californios "could have no respect for his men."

Anti-American feeling rose and on September 23, 1846, 400 Californios under Captain Jose Flores attacked and put Gillespie's band under siege. After three days, Gillespie led his men to a stronger position on a hilltop, but there was no water. Finally, on Sept. 30, outnumbered ten to one, he surrendered. The Mexicans permitted him to march out of San Pedro and board ship. He and his men boarded the *Vandalia* but instead of sailing, they waited for Stockton. Captain Mervine in the *Savannah* rescued Gillespie and his 225 men.

In San Diego, a detachment of the California Battalion had fled to the whaler *Stonington* and was besieged for a month. They were all that remained from the "conquest" of southern California. They were rescued by Lieutenant Archer Gray on the arrival of his 200 sailors and Marines.

In San Francisco, 100 Marines and volunteers led by Marine Captain Marston moved on Santa Clara to punish the rebels. The Mexican leader Francisco Sanchez surrendered and both sides ended up signing an armistice.

Stockton struck back. In October, Navy Captain Mervine led ashore 310 sailors and Marines, plus Gillespie and his force, to attempt the recapture of Los Angeles. The Mexicans set forth a scorched earth policy and moved all the foodstuffs into the interior. On Oct. 8, at Rancho Dominquez, the Americans lost after mounting three failed charges. That night, fast-striking Mexican lancers attacked and by the next afternoon the harassed American expedition had climbed back into its ships.

Late in October, Stockton himself arrived, landing sailors and Marines to hold San Pedro, and sent Gillespie down to San Diego with his own men plus 20 Marines. The men were very poorly armed—a third of them carrying only boarding pikes. The guns of the American warships could hold the ports, but the Mexicans drove the garrison of ten Marines out of Santa Barbara.

Then, word arrived that General Stephen Kearney, guided by Kit Carson, had reached California after a grueling march over mountains and through the Colorado desert. Stockton sent Gillespie and 39 volunteers to meet and reinforce Kearny's troop of 110 men. Later, the Californios said that only the arrival of the Marines had saved Kearny.

The Americans heard that the Californios leader Andris Pico, the Governor's brother, was at the Indian village of San Pasqual. While the American force outnumbered the Mexicans two to one, Kearny's men were totally worn out from the grueling march. At San Pasqual, 100 Mexicans attacked them. With wet ammunition on both sides, the Battle of San Pasqual became a melee between Mexican lances and American sabers. Gillespie's detachment bravely charged but it was a disorganized maneuver due to worn mounts and damp powder.

The Americans got the worst of it. Kearny was lanced twice; Gillespie was thrown from his horse, his saber pinned beneath him. A Californio's lance thrust from the back struck him above his heart, making "a severe gash open to the lungs." Another lancer aimed his weapon at Gillespie's face, cut his upper lip, broke a front tooth, and laid him on his back. Gillespie passed out from loss of blood.

In addition to Kearny's two lance wounds, 22 Americans were killed and 18 more wounded. Some of the Marines had more than eight spear wounds. It was the bloodiest of the battles for California. The Californios had none killed and 12 wounded, but the Americans had held the field. The American dead were buried under a willow tree and the night howled with wolves attracted by the smell. The wounded were carried Indian-style on travois—two stretcher poles dragged behind a horse. They had no fodder for their animals and were short on water as well. Kearny camped at San Bernardo where the men ate mule meat. Capt. Turner sent for help from San Diego and the Army of the West moved westward. Kit Carson, who the Mexicans called *El Lobo*, meaning The Wolf, tried to reach San Diego in advance, walking the 30 miles barefoot through cactus.

Stockton sent 215 Marines and sailors under Lt. Gray to escort Kearny's men to San Diego. The Californios quit tailing the Yankees and melted away.

Then, Stockton set out once again to take Los Angeles by marching 140 miles from San Diego with 600 Marines and sailors.

Fremont moved south with the California Battalion and 428 men. Slaughtering 13 beeves daily, the Marines ate ten pounds of meat per day—the most food they ever had. Fremont camped in the Santa Ynez Mountains and reached Santa Barbara, but Stockton and Kearny moved on Los Angeles without waiting for him to arrive. By this time, the

Mexican Lancers

The Californios' lancers were not like the European trained lancers who came mostly from the upper class. Instead, they were local hide-hunters who went after wild cattle with lances. They were expert horsemen who could ride all day, and could even unsaddle another horse without getting off their own horse. They became very proficient in handling the 12-foot lance, with entire families taking up the art. And lances were cheaper than powder and ball. They used them with great skill and the Marines noticed they always seemed to aim for their kidneys.

Marines' shoes had given out and they wore canvas rags instead, but they reached the San Gabriel River.

Seven miles from Los Angeles, the enemy under Flores, with 500 men and four artillery, made a stand on the bluffs behind the San Gabriel River. The Californios stampeded a herd of wild horses against the American lines and opened fire as the Americans crossed the river.

With Zeilin's Marines holding the right flank, the Americans waded the knee-deep river under fire and charged the enemy. The enemy's front fled, but the Mexican horsemen struck both flanks. The Americans fought, marched, and slept in open squares with their supplies in the center. It was the only way to ward off the lancers. With cannon on each corner of the square spewing grapeshot, the Mexicans were beaten off. That day was the anniversary of the War of 1812's "Battle of New Orleans." It became their battle cry, as the sailors on the left and the Marines on the right took the initiative. The Americans charged up the bluffs and it was over in 90 minutes. Only one American was killed, though this was the Marine Corps' largest battle in California.

1st Lt. Archibald Gillespie,
First U.S.M.C. Special Ops Officer

The Mexicans made one more stand during this two-day running battle, at La Mesa, three miles from the white walls of Los Angeles, in what today is Vernon. Three times the Mexicans charged, but the artillery cut them down. At last, the Mexicans rode off into the mountains, leaving the road to Los Angeles open. Again, Gillespie was wounded. On January 10, with the band playing, Stockton and Kearny led their men into Los Angeles. Gillespie put up the American flag that he had taken down four months earlier. Fremont now entered Los Angeles with a surprise capitulation signed by the Californios at Rancho Cahuenga north of Los Angeles. Kearny's secret orders now became apparent—he revealed that he had orders from Washington to subdue the country, and establish a civil government with himself as the leader. In any event, all of California had finally been conquered.

The conquest taught one important lesson: if the U.S. wanted to extend its concept of Manifest Destiny on hostile coasts, it would need amphibious forces to put ashore. California was finally won when the U.S. could land a force strong enough to hold. The conquest of California was due to the mobility of Stockton's ships and the well-disciplined Marines and seamen of his "gallant sailor army."

Lancers at LaMesa   Artist: Colonel Charles H. Waterhouse, USMCR

Visit the Battlefield: San Pasqual Battlefield State Historic Park, CA State Hwy. 78 (P.M. 25.1)
at Old Pasqual Rd., 7 miles southeast of Escondido

Chapter 23:
Storming the "Halls of Montezuma"

After the Mexican War battle of Churubusco on August 20, 1847, Mexico's General Santa Anna tricked U.S. General Scott into two unfavorable maneuvers. First, he agreed to declare a truce to establish peace negotiations, but this was a ruse. Even while Santa Anna sold supplies to the American invaders, he quietly reinforced his army to 18,000 men while the American force was down to 8,000 effectives.

The second trick was passing false intelligence to Gen. Scott. Santa Anna led Scott to believe that at Molino del Ray, the stronghold west of Mexico City and one mile west of the Hill of Chapultepec, housed a cannon foundry where they were melting brass church bells into heavy cannon. The Americans attacked Molino, and it turned into a costly victory where 750 Americans were killed, and every remaining wounded American was murdered by the Mexicans. After inspection, Scott discovered that there was no foundry there. The heavy losses at Molino brought the six companies of U.S. Marines into battle.

Mexico City was a formidable target. Surrounded by marshes and with approaches via eight causeways, Scott faced obstacles similar to those Cortez had experienced 329 years earlier. Since the southern approach to the capital was heavily fortified, the American plan was to attack from the west at the two *garitos* or gates to the city. Each garito bristled with cannon positioned to rake the roadway. Scott's line then was Molino, then Chapultepec, then the two gates leading into the city. One causeway was the Garita de Belen, another headed north two miles to the Garita de San Cosme.

The Hill of Chapultepec, 200 feet above the surrounding plain, was 600 yards wide, surrounded by a ditch and a 12-foot wall, and topped by a palace that had been made into a military school. It was fortified into a makeshift fortress as the Americans advanced on the capital.

The castle had once been a resort of the Aztec princes. The hill was steep all around except for a slope on the west where the Marines decided to attack. It had a sand-bag barricade at the entryway, and the hillside was mined with charges that were fused to be set off from the fortress.

Generals Scott and Worth regarded the fortress as impregnable. Even though it was vulnerable to American bombardment, both officers were grim on the prospect, and Gen. Worth thought, "we shall be defeated." The hill was a fearsome objective to assault—but if taken, the army would then be able to move onto the causeways leading into the capital.

Two storming parties of 250 men each were assembled. The Marines were assigned to the 4th Division commanded by Army Brigadier General John Quitman, a Mississippian. The Americans moved out of the tree cover and faced the mined hillside that led to the retaining wall of the castle terrace.

At 8 a.m. on Monday, September 13, the attack began. Quitman's men attacked the southern side of Chapultepec. Captain Silas Casey led an assault party of 120 hand-picked soldiers and Marines under Marine Major Levi Twiggs, and 40 Marines commanded by Marine Captain John Reynolds. They faced 1,000 Mexican troops inside the fortress.

The Halls of Montezuma

Chapultepec, also known as "the castle," was an ancient Mexican shrine as well as a recent fortress. Three hundred years before the U.S. war, this had been the summer palace, replete with fountains, of Moctezuma, the Aztec emperor. In 1783, a Spanish viceroy built a new citadel on top of the ruins of the old palace. Surrounded by a huge retaining wall was a broad terrace that made for excellent cannon placement.

Around 1840, the Mexicans made this structure into their National Military Academy. Like at West Point, the young cadets learned military arts in their gray uniforms and tasseled blue caps. About one hundred of the cadets, though ordered to evacuate their school, stayed on and proudly fought to defend this memorial to Mexican history.

Six cadets became the boy heroes of Chapultepec. Those who died were: Vicente Suarez, age 13; Francisco Marquez, 14; Fernando Montes de Ora, 17; Agustin Melgar, 18; Juan de la Barrera, 20; and Juan Escutia, 20.

Cadet Escutia reportedly took the Academy flag from its staff, wrapped it around his body, and valiantly plunged to his death on the rocks below the castle rather than see the flag surrendered to the Americans.

Two of Chapultepec's guns were soon disabled by American battery fire, and the disheartened Mexican soldiers began to desert. From the terrace came a murderous rain of grapeshot and musketry. General Pillow was struck in the ankle, but the whole American force flowed over the redoubt. The Americans were able to cut the canvas powder line that led to the mines and none exploded.

The Marines struggled up the steep southern side, fighting hand-to-hand with bayonets and clubbed rifles. Corporal Hugh Graham and five Marines were killed.

Casey and Twiggs fell wounded, the latter fatally, and they stopped 200 yards short of the guns. Scaling ladders finally reached the Americans. They bridged the ditch and their first wave was mowed down by the Mexicans. So many ladders rose, seemingly at once, that 50 men were up abreast. "And with a shout of victory, the great body of troops rushed over" the walls and gained the castle.

The Americans turned the Mexican guns around, relieving the pressure on Quitman's column. The Mexicans fell back and the Americans charged the castle's main gates. The Mexicans fled so hastily that they "jumped down the eastern side of the rock, regardless of the height."

The young cadets who had refused to desert the school fought to the end. The six boys were killed, as an American correspondent put it, "fighting like demons." They were to be called *Los Ninos Heroicos*—the heroic children.

Mexican officers watching their defeat from a distance said, "God is a Yankee," as Americans from both sides reached the castle. At 9:30 a.m., an American flag was raised over the fortress.

Marine Captain George Terrett led First Lieutenant John Simms, Second Lieutenant Charles Henderson (son of the Commandant), and 36 men to skirt the heights and pursue the retreating enemy northeasterly towards the city itself. Terrett and his Marines raced up the road under heavy fire. Twenty infantry, led by Lieutenant Ulysses S. Grant, the future General and American President, joined them as they fought their way up the San Cosme causeway. They were the spearhead of the army contingent.

Casualties were severe until the Americans remembered the tactic they used at Monterey—breaking their way through the walls of buildings and hauling their guns through them. This tactic also enabled them to fire from the roofs.

General Worth's bugles sounded recall. Terrett went back to report, but Simms and Henderson attacked with 85 men. The gate was too heavily defended to rely on a frontal assault alone, so Marine Lieutenants Simms and Jabez Rich led seven marines to attack from the left. Four were hit. Henderson, wounded in the leg, attacked from the front. Two more men were hit, but together, the two groups seized San Cosme gate as darkness fell.

Worth again sounded recall and the Marines and soldiers withdrew. Six Marines had been killed. Once Chapultepec fell, Quitman moved his division under fire east on the Belen causeway with the Marine battalion right behind a South Carolina regiment. At the Belen gate, they were stopped by enemy fire and Marine Private Tom Kelly was killed. Finally, at 1:20 p.m., the Marines and infantry carried the gate. At dawn on the 14th, Quitman and Worth prepared to assault the city through the two entrances—but Santa Anna had already pulled out.

Though Scott was angry at Quitman for the costliness of his attack on Belen, he felt the Mississippian and his Marines had earned the honor of formally taking the city. Within hours, he would appoint Quitman Mexico City's military governor.

The Americans hardly looked the part of a conquering army. The victorious General Quitman wore only one shoe as he marched at the head of his ragged, blood-stained troops. Only about six thousand Americans remained on their feet—little more than half of those who had left Puebla.

U.S.Marine, 1846
Artist: Colonel Charles H. Waterhouse, USMCR

Quitman's men walked through the crowded streets into the Grand Plaza and took the National Plaza, where before had stood the halls of Montezuma. The Marines were stationed to guard the Palace. The U.S. Marines were now patrolling the halls of Montezuma. In the spring, the veterans were joined by a new 2nd Marine battalion of 367 men commanded by Major John Harris.

On February 2, 1848, the Mexicans accepted peace as the Treaty of Guadalupe Hidalgo was signed. Even though the U.S. was victorious, they agreed to pay Mexico 15 million dollars in cash for the land they coveted. Mexico had lost half her territory—an area larger than France and Germany combined. The American boundary with Mexico would run from the Gulf of Mexico, up the Rio Grande, to the New Mexican border. Then it would continue west to the Pacific at a point one league, or three miles, south of San Diego.

The outspoken Duke of Wellington called Gen. Scott "the greatest living soldier." It had been Scott's flexibility and imagination, his attention to reconnaissance, and his tendency to strike from an unexpected side that supplied the tactics that won the war. In addition, he had the support of solid officers like Thomas (later Stonewall) Jackson, Robert E. Lee, U.S. Grant, P.T. Beauregard and Jefferson Davis. Only 13 years later, all of these men would become major players in the American Civil War.

With this victory, the expansion of the continental United States from coast to coast was now complete. And, in addition to Mexico, the Marines had also captured the opening words to their future Marine Hymn.

The Storming of Chapultepec. Marines attacked on the left slope of the castle.   Artist: Carl Nebel

Visit the Castle: *Museo Nacional de Historia* in Chapultepec Park, Mexico City

Marine Battlefields in North America

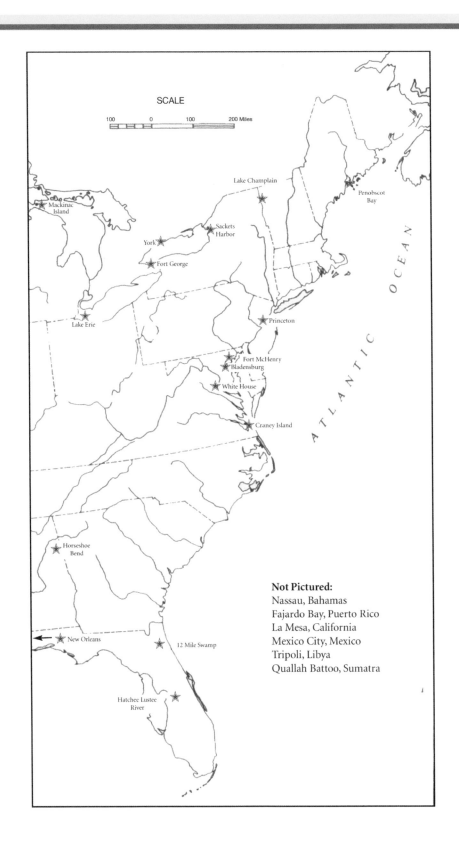

SCALE

100   0   100   200 Miles

Mackinac Island

Lake Champlain

Penobscot Bay

Sackets Harbor

York

Fort George

Lake Erie

Princeton

Fort McHenry
Bladensburg

White House

Craney Island

ATLANTIC OCEAN

Horseshoe Bend

New Orleans

12 Mile Swamp

Hatchee Lustee River

Not Pictured:
Nassau, Bahamas
Fajardo Bay, Puerto Rico
La Mesa, California
Mexico City, Mexico
Tripoli, Libya
Quallah Battoo, Sumatra

Illustrations

Marines Aboard USS Wasp Engage HMS Reindeer. June 1814, by Sgt. John Clymer. (Marine Corps) NARA FILE 127-N-515040

Bugler plays Taps. DoD photo by Mass Communication Specialist 1st Class Chad J. McNeeley/Released. 090311-N-0696M-097

Marine Brigade 1812. Photo courtesy of Don Burzynski. Brooks Detachment: David Krankowski, photographer

Paintings by Colonel Charles Waterhouse, USMCR:

    Placing the Marine Barracks

    First Landing

    Marines with Washington at Princeton

    Assault at Penobscot

    Assault on Derna, Tripoli

    The Final Stand at Bladensburg

    The Battle of New Orleans

    Swamp Ambush

    Foray into Fajardo Bay

    Quallah Battoo

    Lancers at La Mesa

    Messenger of Destiny

Engraved portrait of Commodore Thomas MacDonough, by Alonzo Chappel, 1862. Collection of the author.

Arrival of the American Fleet Prior to the Capture of York. Courtesy of the Toronto Public Library.

Example of American scalp. Courtesy of Bernard J. Lossing.

Painting of Winfield Scott by George Catlin, 1835. This image is in the public domain because its copyright has expired.

Map of Fort George battlefield. Courtesy of Bernard J. Lossing.

Painting of the Battle of Sackets Harbor. Courtesy of Jim Parker

Map of the Battle of Craney Island. Courtesy of Bernard J. Lossing.

Fort Mackinac by Seth Eastman (1808-1875).This image is a work of a U.S. Army soldier or employee, taken or made during the course of the person's official duties. As a work of the U.S. federal government, the image is in the public domain.

Map of the U.S. Forces Attempt to Retake Mackinac Island. Courtesy of Mackinac State Parks.

Battle of Lake Erie, by William Henry Powell, 1865. The work of art is in the public domain because its copyright has expired.

The Niagara Breaks the English Line and The Plight of the Confiance. From paintings by Carlton T. Chapman. From "Naval Actions of The War of 1812," by James Barnes. Copyright 1896, by Harper & Brothers.

Engraved portrait of Commodore Joshua Barney, by Alonzo Chappel, 1862. Collection of the author.

Capture of the City of Washington, based on an engraving from Rapin's History of England, published by J. & J. Gundee, Albion Press, London, 1815.

Engraved portrait of Commodore Thomas MacDonough, by Alonzo Chappel, 1862. Collection of the author.

Potomac River showing earthworks erected by David Porter against the British squadron in September 1814. Courtesy of Fort Belvoir History Department.

Defenders Day fireworks illuminate the Garrison Flag. Photo by Timothy Ervin, National Park Service.

Facsimile of the original manuscript of the first stanza of The Star Spangled Banner. Courtesy of Bernard J. Lossing.

A View of the Bombardment of Fort McHenry. Print by J. Bower.

Battle map of New Orleans, drawn by Gen. Jackson's engineer LaTour, published in 1815. Library of Congress Prints and Photographs Division LC-USZ62-132786. This work is in the public domain because it is a work of the United States Federal Government under the terms of Title 17, Chapter 1, Section 105 of the US Code.

Seminole Chief Osceola (1804–1838), January 1838 by George Catlin, Public Domain.

U.S. Marines searching for the Indians among the mangroves during the Seminole War. Art credit: Defense Dept. Photo (Marine Corps) 306073-A. This image is in the public domain because it contains materials that originally came from the United States Marine Corps, and is a work of the U.S. federal government.

Trail of Tears Map courtesy of Demis and Wilcomb E. Washburn. Handbook of North American Indians. Vol. 4: History of Indian-White Relations. Smithsonian Institution Press, Washington D.C. 1988.

The Storming of Chapultepec by Carl Nebel.

Every effort has been made to acknowledge correctly the source and/or copyright holders of these illustrations, and Warriors Publishing Group apologizes for any unintentional errors or omissions, which will be corrected in future editions.

Bibliography

Barnes, James. *Naval Actions of the War of 1812.* New York, Harper, 1896.

Bauer, K. Jack. *Surfboats and Horse Marines.* Annapolis, US Naval Institute, 1969.

Bennett, M.T. *Lt. Presley Neville O'Bannon*, USMC. Washington, U.S. Marine Corps.

Berton, Pierre. *Flames Across the Border.* Boston, Little Brown, 1981.

Blumenthal, Mark. *Marines of Washington.* Charleston, Arcadia, 2004.

Dunnigan, Brian. "The Battle of Mackinac Island," *Michigan History,* Vol.59 No.4 Winter 1975 239-254.

Cooke, F.O. "O'Bannon in Libya." *Leatherneck Magazine,* August, 1942.

Cruikshank, Lt. Col. Ernest. *The Battle of Fort George.* Niagara-on-the-Lake, Niagara Historical, 1990.

Field, Ron. *The Seminole War,* 1818-1858. Oxford, Osprey, 2009.

Foreman, Grant. *Indian Removal.* Norman, University of Oklahoma, 1932.

Fredrikson, John C. *The War of 1812 in Person.* Jefferson, McFarland, 2010.

Geer, A. "To the Shores." *Leatherneck Magazine,* November, 1952.

Goldowsky, Seebert J. *Yankee Surgeon: The Life and Times of Usher Parsons*, 1788-1868. Boston, Countway, 1988.

Hoffman, Col. Jon T. USMCR. *USMC, A Complete History.* Quantico, Levin, 2002.

King, Grace. *New Orleans: The Place and the People.* New York, Macmillan, 1895.

Latour, Arsene LaCarriere. *Historical Memoir of the War in West Florida and Louisiana in 1812-15.* Gainesville, University Press of Florida, 1999.

Lord, Walter. *The Dawn's Early Light.* Baltimore, John Hopkins University Press, 1972.

Lossing, Bernard J. *Pictorial Field-Book of the War of 1812.* New York, Harper, 1869.

Lyman, Olin L. *Commander Oliver Hazard Perry and the War on the Lakes.* New York, New Amsterdam, 1905.

Martin, M. *History of the Captivity and Sufferings of Mrs. Martin who was Six Years a Captive in Algiers.* Boston, 1807.

McClellan, Maj. Edwin J. USMC *History of the U.S. Marine Corps (Manuscript).* Quantico, Historical Section, 1931.

Millard, James P. "A Signal Victory on Lake Champlain: The Battle of Plattsburg." November 1, 2003 www. Crabisland.com

Millett, Allen R. *Semper Fidelis: The History of the United States Marine Corps.* New York, Macmillan, 1991.

Moskin, J. Robert *The U.S. Marine Corps Story.* New York, Little Brown, 1977.

Nevin, David. *The Mexican War.* Alexandria, Time-Life, 1978.

Phillips, James Duncan. *Pepper and Pirates: Adventures in the Sumutra Pepper Trade of Salem.* Boston, Houghton-Mifflin, 1949.

Pring, Capt. Daniel, RN. "Letter of his Majesty's brig Linnet to Commodore Sir James Yeo, Commander his Majesty's Navy in Canada."

Ray, William, USMC. *Horrors of Slavery or The American Tars in Tripoli.* Troy, 1808

Smith, Charles R. *Marines in the Revolution.* Washington, History and Museums Division Headquarters, USMC, 1975.

Ressler, Sgt. D. Michael. *Historical Perspective on The President's Own U.S. Marine Band.* Washington, History and Museums Division HQ, US Marine Corps, 1988.

Stacey, Col. C.P. *The Battle of Little York.* Toronto, Toronto Historical, 1977.

Tucker, Glen. *Dawn Like Thunder: The Barbary Wars and the Birth of the U.S. Navy.* Indianopolis, Bobbs-Merrill, 1963.

Waterhouse, Col. Charles. *Marines and Others.* Edison, Sea Bag, 1994.

Wilder, Patrick A. *The Battle of Sackett's Harbor.* Baltimore, Nautical and Aviation, 1994.

Author, Don Burzynski

Don Burzynski was a guest history columnist for the Marine Corps Times and Navy Times in Arlington. He has been a historian for 52 years starting as a re-enactor in 1959, reliving the Civil War Centennial, the Bi-Centennial of the American Revolution and currently the Bi-Centennial of the War of 1812.

He holds three Detroit EMMYs and two CLIOs for commercial concepts when he was a Creative Director/Producer in the advertising field.

He has spoken and conducted research for The History Channel and has appeared in a number of their films. In 1996, he won the prestigious Magruder Award from the Marine Corps Historical Foundation for living history excellence.

This is Don's first book on the U.S. Marines and he has begun a volume on The Sea Soldiers in the War of 1812

This book was made possible by a research grant from the Marine Corps Historical Foundation.

Illustrations by Colonel Charles Waterhouse, USMC (Retired)

During his long career, Col. Charles Waterhouse has served in the ranks of both Marines and others. The first tour of duty as a Marine was in 1943-46 with the 5th Marine Division Fleet Marine Force in the Pacific during World War II. The second tour was from 1972-92 as artist-in-residence, USMC. The years in between and since have been spent as artist and illustrator for major book and magazine publishers, advertising, and private clients, and as official or combat artist for all services.

Colonel Waterhouse has graciously offered his wonderful illustrations for this first ever book on The First Leathernecks.

10979845R00073

Made in the USA
Charleston, SC
21 January 2012